The Big Five Forces of Business

A mental model for successful organizations

Allan N. Ebedes

To my loving family, who gives me so much joy and pride.

To Heddy, my wonderful wife of over forty years.

To our incredible children and grandchildren: Mark, Risa, Hailey, Brandon, and Evan; Nicole, Bram, and Aaron; Gavin and Jacki; Lauren and Jordan; and to any future grandchildren with whom we may be blessed.

In loving memory of my late parents, Harry and Micky Ebedes, who taught me that education is the best investment that one can make, as it can never be taken away.

Other Works by Allan N. Ebedes

Your LifePlan

10 "F-Words" for Your Life

You Got It! How to Deliver Superb Customer Service

Contents

Introduction

Overview of The Big Five Forces

Do you ever feel overwhelmed by business information?

Are you:
- Inundated with articles in business newspapers and newsletters from the latest business gurus?
- Unable to keep up with the latest authors of business books on every topic imaginable?
- Overwhelmed by a multitude of business magazines, business journals, and ground-breaking academic theories from Ivy League business schools?
- Confused by too many buzzwords?
- Drowning in too much information (TMI)?
- Tired of the latest "flavour of the week" solutions and "secrets of success" that others claim to be able to unlock?

There are literally thousands of programs, seminars, courses, and webinars offered every day on every business topic from A to Z (see the sample list of topics in Appendix A.)

Sometimes business trends seem like the latest fad diets or nutrition programs. Should you eat no carbs or lots of carbs? Should you eat little protein or all protein? Are fruits and vegetables good for you? Are starches good for you? Is coffee good or bad for you? Do you ever say to yourself, "Surely the doctors, nurses, dieticians, nutritionists, and government health ministries can agree on what is healthy or not, and come up with the ideal diet of what foods to eat and what to avoid."

It's easy to feel the same way about business books, knowledge, and information. Today there are millions of websites, thousands of software programs and applications, and hundreds of communication devices that, through high-speed internet, web browsers, and search engines, give us access to all the knowledge and information that exists in the world. All we have to do is make the appropriate keystrokes on our desktops (so 2000!), laptops, smartphones, and tablets.

Consider social media, which did not exist just a few years ago. You risk being called a dinosaur if you are not on Facebook, LinkedIn, Twitter, Foursquare, Instagram, and the like. And it is nearly impossible to engage efficiently in social media—and do business—without that aforementioned smartphone.

Even if you are comfortable with all this innovation in technology, speed-of-light communication, and access to knowledge, you are more likely to succeed *in business* if you remain aware of a few universal, evergreen, and unchanging business principles. As a businessperson, entrepreneur, leader, or manager, you need a mental model for thinking strategically and holistically about how best to operate and grow your business or organization. My book attempts to build you a framework for a common-sense, consistent, clear, and comprehensive mental model.

Why do I feel that I am qualified to present this framework? For over forty years, I have been an ardent "student of business." I have earned four business degrees, two at the master's level. I have been an employee, an accountant, an entrepreneur, a founder, a businessman, a president, a CEO, a lecturer, a teacher, and a mentor. I believe that I have been relatively successful in a variety of careers and businesses in diverse fields including public accounting, retail furniture and appliances, retail computer hardware and software, computer distribution, career training and adult education, the restaurant industry, and the not-for-profit sector. I founded and built a chain of fifty career colleges, coast-to-coast across Canada, that have provided an education to over a quarter of a million adults. I have lectured to fourth-year college students majoring in accounting, and I have facilitated corporate-training workshops on numerous soft-skill and hard-skill topics. I have mentored entrepreneurs, taken a company public through an IPO on the NASDAQ stock exchange, and served on various boards of directors.

I have attended hundreds of business conferences, courses, seminars, and webinars, listened to umpteen speakers and "gurus" on the latest business trends and ideas, and read hundreds of books by great authors (see the bibliography at the end of this book) and thousands of business magazines and newspapers. While taking in the advice of all of these pundits, I undertook to devise a simple system to help a C-suite executive, a business leader, manager, owner, or entrepreneur to focus on the critical aspects that apply to every business. While I have learned a tremendous amount from books and lecturers, I believe that my personal business experiences, successes, and failures— and there have been many—position me to share my mental model for business success.

I have always enjoyed books that can be read from cover to cover on a short flight or while commuting to work on a train. So I intentionally kept this book short so that it can be read in a couple of hours. It is also written without too many examples or long narratives and descriptions, because the points are intended to be self-explanatory. It is written in plain language with few buzzwords. It is not intended to be an academic monograph.

My goal is to make this book as simple and as straightforward as possible. If, after reading it, you feel that you did not learn anything new, I will not be offended in the least. But I hope that you will feel that the mental model rings true to your personal business experience, and that it will serve as a useful, top-of-the-mind framework to help you and your team focus on what is really important in the day-to-day heat of the battle of business, where you are striving to survive and thrive, grow and prosper.

It has been said that business is too complicated to have simple solutions. While I acknowledge that greater sophistication must often be brought to bear on business problems by executives and professionals such as accountants, lawyers, tax specialists, consultants, economists, and academics, too often one can become bedazzled by the complexity of such expertise and "take one's eye off the ball."

I welcome your feedback and opinions after you have read this book. Please tell me whether you have found it useful as a mental model. You can reach me by e-mail at: allan@managementmentors.ca.

An Evergreen Framework or Mental-Model

This book offers a mental model that is simple to remember, logical, and applicable to any business or organization, large or small, no matter the industry or sector. And the framework won't change from year to year, nor will it become outdated or irrelevant over time. At the same time, it is dynamic enough to be able to accommodate the latest thinking and ideas, because business and the economy are dynamic, and change is constant due to innovation, technology, and the next generation of business and thought-leaders.

One doesn't need to reinvent the wheel. The wheel is one of the greatest inventions of all time. Like the discovery of fire, the invention of the Gutenberg printing press, and the development of the integrated circuit and computer chip, the wheel changed everything. But since its invention, the wheel hasn't changed that much.

The following illustration displays the mental model, titled The Big Five Forces of Business.

Each of the Big Five Forces starts with the letter *P* for ease of recall, namely:

1. Purpose
2. Purchasers
3. People
4. Planning
5. Performance

I could also have easily added several more important *P*'s to the framework such as: Policies and Procedures, Processes, Project Management, Performance Management, Process Management, Problem-Solving, Products, Programs, Partners, Progress, Predictability, Proactivity, Prospecting, Profitability, Principles, Prudence, Planet, and Passion, to name but a few. But this would have made the model too complex and too difficult to remember. And in any event, as will be seen, all of these other *P*'s are really subsets of the Big Five Forces.

As I touched upon previously, I apply the term "business" not only to large and small corporations, partnerships or sole proprietorships, but also to not-for-profit organizations (hospitals, schools, charities, etc.), to governments (federal, provincial/state, and municipal) and departments, and generally to all organizations and enterprises that sell or provide products or services to individuals or to other businesses.

Furthermore, it matters not if the business is a start-up or is already in existence and well established, as the principles of the Five Forces apply equally to all of them. And the businesspeople referred to in this book may be owner/shareholders, hired-gun managers, or government employees.

Why the Big *Five*?

Anyone who has ever gone on a safari or vacation in a wildlife-game park such as those located in South Africa (where I was born) will know that the goal is to see the "big five" animals, namely, lions, leopards, elephants, buffalo, and rhinoceroses. Sure, you will see zebras, giraffes, hippopotamuses, hyenas, and kudus. But unless you see the "Big Five," your wildlife safari will be incomplete, and you may feel lost. The same applies to business. There are many ways to "make a buck," but without the Big Five Forces, you may go astray on your business journey.

Chapter 1

Force One: Purpose

Every business and organization needs to be very clear about the purpose for which it was founded and continues to exist. What is the purpose of your business or organization? This may seem like a very straightforward and simple question, but it is really a profound and fundamental question that needs to be answered clearly and concisely. The answer needs to be much more specific than a statement like "to make money" or "to serve the customer" or "to look after a patient" or "to teach students," and so on. In a business or organization, purpose—the reason for an entity's very existence—is often referred to as the *mission* of the organization.

Mission

The Purpose or Mission Statement should answer the following questions:

Whose mission is it? Does it belong to the whole business or organization (e.g., an entire corporation) or just a department or unit (e.g., the marketing department of a business or a police department) within the organization?
What does the organization or department do?
What is the nature of the business?
Whom does the organization serve? That is, who are its stakeholders? Examples of stakeholders include purchasers, customers, clients, citizens, patients, students, shareholders, and employees.
Why does the organization or business serve the identified stakeholders? In other

words, what benefit(s) do the stakeholders derive?

How does the organization carry out its mission? Aspects to be considered here include quality, timeliness, value, cost-effectiveness, safety, and so forth.

Purpose provides guidance to the management team not just about what it should do, but, just as importantly, what it should not do as well. It requires discipline to stop doing what does not fit in with an organization's mission or is at odds with its values (see Values, below). Even a tempting, great opportunity is not necessarily worth pursuing if it does not fit the mission.

Of course, over time, a business must make a profit by selling products and/or services to purchasers, its customers. (See chapter 2, "Force Two: Purchasers.") The statement of purpose needs to be clear about what these products and services are, whether they will be produced by the business or by a third party, and whether the business will serve as the manufacturer/producer, distributor, or retailer of these products and services.

A not-for-profit organization, of which there are millions, is not concerned so much with making money as with helping to improve the lives of the purchasers of its services. The purchasers may be members of the organization, beneficiaries of a charity, or patients in a hospital, among others.

However, in both for-profit businesses and not-for-profit organizations, the purpose or mission must be meaningful and compelling enough for stakeholders to believe in it. It is the primary responsibility of the business or organization leaders to make sure that all the stakeholders know, understand, and buy into the purpose. They must be able to feel that what they do every day contributes to the purpose and to be proud of their contribution.

Many organizations and most Fortune 500 companies have clear mission statements. They are often framed and hung in reception areas and boardrooms, printed on the backs of business cards, displayed on their websites and in other promotional materials.

The term "mission" derives from the military, where the commanding officers need to clearly communicate to the troops what their "mission" is, as in "Our mission is to capture the enemy artillery bunker on the hill using paratroopers and commandos." Note that the mission in this example is very specific. It is not a broad statement, such as "Our mission is to win the war," which would not be very useful to the troops on the ground. Unfortunately, too many business mission statements of businesses are so vague that they could apply to almost any business. For example, here are some mission statements that, while short and punchy, are so generic that they don't define the respective purposes of their specific businesses.

Can you tell which organizations these mission statements belong to? (The answers are given below.)

a. To provide a better work experience.

b. Helping our customers succeed.

c. Our mission is to deliver superior quality products and services for our customers and communities through leadership, innovation, and partnerships.

d. Simpler, Faster, Better...Together.

e. To simply delight you...every day.

f. To serve patients.

Here are some examples of more specific Mission Statements. Which companies do you think they relate to? (The answers are given below.)

g. At [...] we work to help people and businesses throughout the world realize their full potential. This is our mission. Everything we do reflects this mission and the values that make it possible.

h. To bring inspiration and innovation to every athlete in the world. "If you have a body, you are an athlete."

i. Dedication to the highest quality of customer service, delivered with a sense of warmth, friendliness, individual pride, and company spirit.

j. Our strategic intent is to help people find better ways to do great work—by constantly leading in document technologies, products, and services that improve our customers' work processes and business results.

k. Together we will build the world's most extraordinary food company.

l. We exist to benefit and refresh everyone it [sic] touches.

m. We will earn the loyalty of our guests by consistently exceeding their expectations for personal service and warm hospitality and by welcoming them in distinctive surroundings.

n. Nourishing Families. Enriching Lives.

o. To be a source of excellence for our customers; to provide a challenging work experience for our employees; to be a rewarding investment for our shareholders; to be a respected citizen of community and country.

Answers to quiz:

a. Steelcase
b. Sysco
c. Wendy's
d. Armstrong Wood Industries
e. Sara Lee Corporation
f. Amgen
g. Microsoft
h. Nike
i. Southwest Airlines
j. Xerox
k. Campbell Soup
l. Coca-Cola
m. Fairmont Hotels
n. Del Monte
o. Sunoco

One should not confuse a mission statement with an advertising tag line, which is a slogan that is designed to create a brand identity. Here are several tag lines used by some well-known companies:

"Save money. Live better." (Walmart)

"We sell for less every day." (Walmart)

"We do it all for you." (McDonald's)

"You deserve a break today." (McDonald's)

"You're richer than you think." (Scotiabank)

"Always fresh." (Tim Horton's)

"Things are brighter under the sun." (Sun Life Financial)

"Good to the last drop." (Maxwell House)

"Just do it." (Nike)

"Put a tiger in your tank." (Esso)

"Snap! Crackle! Pop!" (Kellogg's Rice Krispies)

"Reach out and touch someone." (Bell)

"It tastes awful, but it works." (Buckley's)

"Don't leave home without it." (American Express)

"M'm! M'm! Good!" (Campbell's)

The key point is that the mission statement is not just a marketing slogan. It should clearly and concisely state the purpose of the business and drive its strategic business plan. (See chapter 4, "Force Four: Planning, below.) It should tell where the organization is headed, the position it intends to stake out, and the capabilities it plans to develop.

All employees should know why they come to work at the business every day and why they receive their pay cheques. All customers should know what to expect from that business.

A mission/purpose statement should convey the reason why the business exists in as few words as possible. It should answer the question, "What are you trying to do and for whom?" When developing a mission statement, it is advisable to use the KISS principle: **K**eep **I**t **S**imple and **S**traightforward. Everyone should be able to read, understand, and remember the mission statement.

The mission statement will shape your organization's culture and the behaviours of the people in your organization. It explains why you do what you do (but not necessarily how you do it). When you craft the mission statement, consider the needs and wants of your customers, the purchasers of your products and services (see chapter 2, "Force Two: Purchasers"). After all, customers are the people who make your business successful. You should also involve as many stakeholders as possible in composing the statement. People at different levels of the organization may have diverse and beneficial insights to offer. Even individuals from outside your organization may be involved, to provide feedback. Use a network of colleagues and experts to solicit objective input, making sure the individuals you select understand your business and the competitive environment.

When writing the mission statement, remember that less is more. Statements that are too long and wordy—especially those that run over several paragraphs—are almost impossible for people to internalize and remember, let alone be inspired by. Let your mission statement be short enough to fit on a T-shirt.

Once you have a draft of your mission statement, run it by all stakeholders; make sure they understand it and deem it simple enough to be memorable. Remember to thank all the individuals who made an effort to contribute to the development of the purpose/mission statement. While their specific words may not have been adopted, let them know that, at least in spirit, their contributions were critical to the final version.

As soon as your mission statement is agreed upon and committed to writing, you should begin to market it with vigour. Distribute it throughout the organization. Post it on your corporate website. Make colourful and graphical posters with the mission statement printed on them and post them around the business. Print the mission statement on the back of business cards and show it proudly on promotional materials. Have contests among your staff to check for comprehension. The mission statement will have no value if it is written and then simply filed away, never to be looked at again.   To ensure that the mission statement is top-of-the-mind, one criterion in performance evaluation could be how well employees adhere to and contribute to the organization's mission and purpose.

It is important to note that, ultimately, the purpose or mission of an organization is not cast in stone. Business is dynamic and change is constant; a business's will change over time as it enters new markets, creates new products, or exits certain initiatives. When such a change happens, the mission statement needs to be revised and updated to clearly reflect current purpose in the current business environment. In fact, it is best to review the mission statement periodically to ensure that it still reflects the nature of the business.

Ongoing analysis of the mission is critical and will be discussed in more detail under "Force Four: Planning" (chapter 4). When you begin to develop the business plan, you should be able to use what you have learned in crafting the mission and have the plan reaffirm it. If the two do not match, you may need to revisit and revise the mission. But in the final analysis, the real test is not how clever the purpose or mission statement is or reads, but the quality of results achieved by the business or organization. (See chapter 5, "Force Five: Performance," below).

In addition to (and in connection with) being constantly aware of the true nature of your business and the identity of your stakeholders, you should consider the following questions:

1. What factors are critical to your success?
2. What are your organization's strengths, weaknesses, opportunities, and threats (SWOT)?
3. What are your challenges?

4. What values and principles must guide your business? (See Values, below.)
5. What fundamental policy decisions do you need to make?
6. What actions will be necessary to implement those policies?
7. What are your priorities?
8. What resources will you need in the way of people, equipment, money, and time, among others?

Many businesses transformed into very different companies over time. Some examples are the following:

- 3M was Minnesota Mining and Manufacturing before becoming a company focused on adhesive products.
- IBM has become more of a services company than a computer-hardware company.
- Apple transformed itself by innovation from selling just desktop computers to its highly successful iPods, iTunes, iPhones and iPads.
- McDonald's, while still selling burgers, fries, and shakes, has added food items such as chicken, salads, deli-sandwiches, muffins, and coffee to its menu.
- Tim Horton's has expanded its products from primarily coffee and donuts to include bagels, soups, breakfast items, yogurt, and chicken sandwiches. And it is now taking on more of the qualities of Starbucks.

Whenever an organization is making a strategic decision, it is important to review the current mission statement, so that decisions will align with it. Strategic business decisions, not only by top management, but by all employees throughout the organization, should only be made after a review of the mission statement and what the organization stands for.

Having a clearly defined purpose for the business or organization is essential to ensure that owners, management, and staff focus on the reason the business or organization exists. It is very easy to get side-tracked or pulled off-course in pursuit of other activities, projects, and initiatives that do not contribute to the core business purpose. Of course, if other opportunities present themselves that management feels would be lucrative, then they should consider them. But first they should do an in-depth evaluation of how the new venture(s) will impact the current business. If the impact is deemed positive, then the enterprise's mission statement should be revised to reflect this new direction.

As mentioned, Apple was originally only in the computer business. But as a result of the vision of Steve Jobs, Apple entered into the portable-music business with its innovative MP3 player, called an iPod, and iTunes, which allowed users to legally download music for just ninety-nine cents a song rather than illegally downloading copyrighted songs. This became an enormous business and profit centre for Apple with hundreds of millions of paid downloads. And the iPod led to the development of the iPhone, which became the biggest selling smartphone, taking over the market supremacy that BlackBerry had once enjoyed. Of course, Apple's advancements led to new competition, namely, Google's Android operating system, on which platform Samsung has at the time of this writing become the largest-selling smartphone company.

Apple's purpose had changed from selling just computers to innovating and developing cool gadgets for the consumer. Apple then created a brand-new product category that consumers didn't even know they needed or wanted with the introduction of a tablet computer, the iPad, which far outstripped the sales from its original PC business.

The point is that while it is important to be focused on

the current purpose of the business, the business cannot put on blinders to new opportunities. Often spinoff products, or new business ventures that arise from the existing enterprise, can either be more profitable than the original business purpose, or require a redefinition of that purpose. Apple changed from selling cool computers to the creation of cool, innovative, electronic gadgets and products, and consumers would stand in line for many hours just to be among the first to buy them.

Therefore, focus combined with flexibility, are the keys to long-term success.

Vision

In addition to the mission statement, it is customary for an organization to also create a Vision Statement. The vision statement is like an extended weather forecast; it seeks to tell stakeholders what the business aspires to become in the long term. Whereas a mission statement reflects the "nuts and bolts" of the business, a vision statement should be aspirational and inspirational; it should motivate stakeholders to join or support the business's cause.

An example of an inspirational vision statement would be the speech given by President John. F. Kennedy on May 25, 1961, when he announced before a special joint session of Congress the dramatic and ambitious goal of sending an American safely to the moon before the end of the decade. In his speech he laid out the following vision: "We plan on sending a man to the moon by the end of the decade and bring him back safely to earth. We choose to do so, not because it is easy, but because it is hard."

The decision involved much consideration before it was made public; enormous human efforts and expenditures went into making what became Project Apollo a reality by 1969. Only the construction of the Panama Canal in modern peacetime and the Manhattan Project in wartime were comparable in scope. NASA's overall human-spaceflight efforts were guided by Kennedy's speech; projects Mercury (at least in its latter stages), Gemini, and Apollo were designed to execute Kennedy's goal. That goal was achieved on July 20, 1969, when Apollo 11 commander Neil Armstrong stepped off the lunar module's ladder and onto the moon's surface.

When Kennedy made that speech, it was not physically possible to send a man to the moon. NASA didn't have the rocket fuel-cells that were needed, the computer capability was not yet developed, and there were numerous other technological challenges. But the vision of sending a man to the moon motivated the entire nation and mobilized America's race for space supremacy. It also brought on the development of technology that would, as it turned out, benefit more than just the space program.

A vision Statement should inspire the desire by employees to work for the company, by shareholders to invest in it, and by suppliers to do business with it. By identifying what the company would like to achieve or accomplish, a good vision statement provides the inspiration for the daily operations of a business and molds its strategic decisions.

Aspirational in nature, vision statements lay out the most important primary goals for companies. Generally, they don't outline plans for achieving those goals. But by outlining the key objectives for a company, they enable the company's employees to develop business strategies to achieve the stated goals. A single unifying vision statement motivates employees to be more productive.

Here are examples of motivating vision statements:

- The Princess Margaret Cancer Foundation: To conquer cancer in our lifetime.
- National Multiple Sclerosis Society: A World Free of MS.
- Habitat for Humanity: A world where everyone has a decent place to live.
- Cleveland Clinic: Striving to be the world's leader in patient experience, clinical outcomes, research and education.

Here are examples of vision statements of a few well-known, for-profit companies:

- Toys "R" Us: To put joy in kids' hearts and a smile on parents' faces.
- Avon: To be the company that best understands and satisfies the product, service and self-fulfillment needs of women—globally.
- Amazon: Our vision is to be Earth's most customer-centric company; to build a place where people can come to find and discover anything they might want to buy online.
- Kraft: Helping people around the world eat and live better.
- McDonald's: To be the world's best quick-service restaurant experience. Being the best means providing outstanding quality, service, cleanliness, and value, so that we make every customer in every restaurant smile.
- Nike: To bring inspiration and innovation to every athlete in the world. If you have a body, you are an athlete.
- Harley-Davidson: To provide extraordinary motorcycles and customer experiences.

- DuPont: Creating sustainable essentials to a better, safer and healthier life for people.

The difference between a purpose/mission statement and a vision statement is that the mission states what the business is striving to achieve right now. The vision however, is something that the business hopes to achieve in the future.

Values

In addition to having a mission statement and a vision statement, it is also beneficial for a business to be clear about its core values. Values or principles determine how the organization will conduct itself without compromise or variation, no matter how its purpose may change over time. Clarity about core values is important to ensure that the stakeholders stay true to their beliefs about how the business does business. Values guide the management and staff in how they will conduct business and treat each other and their customers, suppliers, and other stakeholders. Values are like the North Star: they shouldn't change direction over time.

When you undertake to compose concise and meaningful mission and vision statements and establish core values for your business or organization, try to do so away from the office—perhaps at a retreat—so that your ad hoc team does not become distracted by day-to-day business interruptions. The engagement of an experienced facilitator to help guide your team in this work is invaluable and is highly recommended.

When doing a values exercise, it is useful for all the members of the cross-functional team of, say, ten to twenty people to write down, on sheets of paper or Post-it Notes, one or two words for important values that they believe should guide the organization now and in the future. The facilitator should record these values on flip-chart paper and pin those sheets up on the walls around the room. If, for example, there are fifteen participants in the team and each person lists ten values, then there may be as many as 150 values listed on the flip charts. Clearly, no organization can be guided by so many values. Shoot for and whittle down to no more than the "Ten Commandments" or thereabouts for the business.

Usually two or more persons express common values; the words they use may differ but have the same intent nonetheless. For example, words such as "trust," "integrity," and "honesty" may all mean essentially the same thing; the team should choose just one of these. Similarly, expressions such as "teamwork," "cooperation," "rowing the boat in the same direction," and "singing from the same song sheet" all convey a common value, and the team should vote for one word or phrase.

However, in the negotiating and trade-off process of getting the list down to between six and ten values, remember that just because a value doesn't make the short list, does not mean that it is not important. For example, if integrity or teamwork doesn't make the final list, this does not mean that it is acceptable that people are dishonest or undermine each other.

Often Values are listed so as to create an easily remembered acronym. For example, at Excellence Canada the values are:

People

Relationships

Integrity

Dedication

Excellence

As can be seen, the first letters of the values spell the word "pride."

North York General Hospital displays posters on all its floors listing the following "patient values":

Respect

Equity

Safety

Patient-focus

Excellence

Communication

Trust

The first letters spell the word "respect." North York General Hospital also has a statement spelling "integrity":

Integrity

Nurturing

Teamwork

Excellence

Growth

Respect

Initiative

Trust

You

When crafting statements of mission, vision and values, it is useful to have a checklist of possible keywords to choose from, such as the following, listed alphabetically:

A. accomplishment, accountability, accurate, achievement, action, adaptable, advance, advanced, affirmation, affordable, agile, alignment, ambitious, anchor, appreciation, aspiration, aspire, asset, attainment, attitude, attractive, authentic, autonomy, awards

B. balanced, beacon, beautiful, believe, benefit, best, better, bold, bond, brand, build, business

C. caring, celebrate, celebration, challenges, challenging, change, character, cheap, citizens, clean, coach, collaboration, commitment, commitments, communication, community, compassion, competent, competitive, competitors, concerned, confidence, connectivity, consistency, constant, consumer, continuous improvement, conviction, cost-effective, courage, create, creativity, credo, CSR, culture, customer

D. dedication, delight, deliver, demonstrate, determination, develop, difference, differentiate, dignity, discipline, disruption, distinction, distinctive, diversity, dynamic

E. earn, economical, educational, effective, efficacy, efficient, empathy, employees, employment, empower, empowerment, enable, encourage, energy, engaged, enrich, enthusiasm, enthusiastic, entrepreneurial, entrepreneurship, environmental, equality, ethical, exceed, excel, excellence, exceptional, excitement, expand, expectations, experience, expertise

F. failure, fairness, family, faster, financial, first, flexibility, focus, focused, foundation, freedom, friendly, fun, future

G. game plan, generous, global, goal-oriented, goals, Golden Rule, good works, goodwill, graciousness, growth, guiding principles

H. happiness, hard work, harmony, health, heart, helping, heritage, high performance, high-tech, history, honesty, honour, human, humanity

I. ideals, ideas, ideology, impress, improve, increase, independence, individuals, information, initiative, innovation, inspiration, inspire, integrity, intent, investment, invigorate, involved

J. jobs, joy, just, justice, just in time

K. Kaizen, keep promises, kindness, knowledge

L. leader, leadership, lean, learning, life, lifestyle, listening, lives, long term, loyalty

M. market leadership, members, mentorship, mission, most respected, motivated, mutual respect, mutuality

N. nature, needs, neighbourly, never-say-never, new, nimbleness, nourishing

O. objectives, obligation, one-stop, openness, opportunity, organizational excellence, outreach, outsource

P. participative, partners, passion, peace of mind, people, performance, perseverance, personal growth, planet, positive, positive people, positivity, potential, power, powerful, predictability, preeminent, preferred, premier, preserve, preserving, pride, principles, priorities, proactive, processes, productivity, products, professional, professionalism, profit, profitability, progress, progressive, promises, provider, prudence, purpose, push

Q. qualified, quality, quantity, quest for excellence

R. reality, reasonable, recognition, redefine, relationships, relentless, reliable, renewal, resources, respect, responsible, responsive, results, return, reward, rewarding, right thing, risk, risk-taking

S. safety, satisfaction, security, self-assessment, self-respect, service, sharing, smarter, social, society, solutions, speed, spirit, stakeholders, stand for something, standards, stewardship, stimulate, strategy, strengths, strive, structure, success, superior, sustainable

T. talent, team, teamwork, technologies, think outside the box, thoughtful, timeliness, togetherness, top-performing, total, training, transform, transparency, trust, truth, turbulent

U. unique, unity, urgency, urgent, useful

V. valuable, value, values, vision

W. warmth, waste reduction, wealth, wellness, winning, wisdom, work hard, world-class, worth

X. eXtraordinary

Y. yes-we-can-attitude, you

Z. zeal, zen, zest, zippy

In the final analysis, the core values that you have agreed upon for your business or organization should govern everything that you do. And anyone should be able to question senior management if decisions or actions violate these values. For example, if "teamwork" is a value, then a manager should not expect his employees to be working overtime or on weekends while he goes golfing. And if "integrity" is a value, everyone should be held accountable to ensure that no one violates this key principle by misleading or misrepresenting to customers or employees. If "customer service" is a core value, then everyone from the C-suite down to the front lines should be expected to do everything possible to satisfy customers.

Principles

In addition to establishing core values, it is also useful for the organization to develop guiding principles, which are beliefs that will help to govern the direction of the organization. Examples of Principles are:

- We believe that our strength lies in our people. Accordingly we will endeavour to hire the best possible team members, provide them with extensive training, and foster a healthy workplace culture where we work hard but also have fun together.
- We believe in Corporate Social Responsibility (CSR) and giving back to the community, so every employee will have three paid days off a year to contribute to agreed-upon community initiatives such as United Way, Habitat for Humanity, or other charities and good deeds that the team shall determine.

We believe it is our duty to contribute to the protection of the environment and planet earth, and accordingly we will follow best practices for the three R's: reducing, recycling, and reusing. We will conserve energy by installing energy-efficient lighting and using energy-efficient equipment.

Force One: Purpose

Summary

The first step for any business or organization, whether it's a start-up or a well-established enterprise, is to be clear about its purpose. What is its current mission? What is its vision for the future? What values and principles will guide the management and team of the business?

This "first step" should be readdressed at least annually by any business or organization. Just as you would make an appointment with your dentist every four to six months for a check-up or take your car in for a service and oil change two or three times a year, so should you perform a regular check-up on your business to ensure that the goals, strategies, tactics, and actions of your team are congruent with the purpose of the business.

"If you don't know where you are going, any road will get you there," goes the old saying. Purpose is the first principle in The Big Five Forces of Business; it ensures that the business knows where it is going and which road to take to get there.

Action Items:

1. Craft a clear and concise **Purpose** or Mission statement for your business or organization.
2. Review your Purpose at least annually as the nature of the business can change over time. "The main thing is to ensure that the main thing is, in fact, still the main thing"!
3. Dream about what your business could become in ten or twenty years by drafting a **Vision Statement** that is both aspirational and motivating.

4.   Decide what **Values** will be your North-Star and guide the way you and your team conduct business.
5.   Determine the guiding **Principles** that will help govern the direction of the organization

Chapter 2

Force Two: Purchasers

The second of the Big Five Forces in the mental model is made up of "purchasers." Purchasers are most commonly referred to as "customers," but I have used the word "purchasers" instead for several reasons. The first is pedagogical; obviously I want the term to match the other P's in the mental model and make the Five Forces easier to remember.

Second, purchasers may not necessarily be the end users of the products or services. A purchaser can merely be the person or business or department that is making the buying decision. The purchaser may or may not be responsible for paying for the product or service. This would most commonly happen in large corporations or governments or in the military, where there are departments that are responsible for procurement for other departments. Customers, whether internal or external, are usually also the consumers of the products and services, which is not necessarily the case with purchasers.

Third, using the term "purchasers" also highlights the fact that no sale is ever made until someone actually agrees to purchase the products or services being sold by the seller. The mission of the business or organization is unlikely to be fulfilled unless someone actually buys its products or services.

Fourth, the purchase of any product or service can also be the result of influence by different parties such as initiators, influencers, decision makers, and the buyer. For example, the decision to purchase a new home may have been initiated by a friend who just bought a new home; the children may be influencers as to the neighbourhood schools. The ultimate decision-maker may be the mother while the father may be responsible for making the mortgage payments. Similarly, the decision to buy a new family car may be influenced by neighbours, determined by the needs of the children and the dad's desire for a new, cool SUV, and finalized by the practical argument to buy a minivan being made by the mother.

There is no sector of the economy from which purchasers are absent. Purchasers do business with all of the following entities, among others:

- Manufacturers, who sell the goods they have manufactured to purchasers who may be other manufacturers for inputs, distributors, wholesalers, or even large retailers such as Walmart, Target, and Home Depot.
- Mining companies, who sell their mined iron ore, zinc, platinum, diamonds, gold, and so forth, to smelters, precious metal exchanges, and the like.
- Farmers, who sell their crops, livestock, or the output of that livestock (e.g., eggs and milk) through marketing co-ops, meat producers, produce markets, or large food processors.
- Builders, who sell houses, factories, office buildings, and other structures either to developers or directly to the end user.
- Professionals such as lawyers, accountants, management consultants, investment advisors, stock brokers, architects, interior designers, engineers, and realtors, who sell their specialized knowledge and expertise.
- Doctors, dentists, hospitals, nurses and other specialists in the medical industry, who sell their expertise to patients. Patients may not pay for them

directly, however; fees may be paid by government health plans or by insurance companies.

- Schools, colleges and universities, who sell education and training. Either students or their families pay for these services directly or they obtain government student loans that will need to be paid back.
- Governments (federal, provincial or municipal), who provide services to citizens/residents in exchange for taxes.

The point of the above examples is that the efficient functioning and growth of the economy depends upon individuals, businesses, and governments purchasing products and services. Governments set economic policy based upon the level of purchasing, consumption, and investing activity that is taking place in the economy, which creates jobs and employment. If there is too much activity (or, in economic terms, demand exceeds supply, or there is too much money chasing too few goods), then this can lead to inflation, and the Central Bank or Federal Reserve tries to control inflation through regulations, the setting of interest rates, and other monetary-policy tools. This book, however, is not about macroeconomics. Suffice it to say for our purposes that purchasers and purchasing power are essential for all businesses and the economy.

Clearly, if the purpose of a business is to be realized, purchasers must be primed to buy its products and services on an ongoing basis. As we have seen, depending on the industry or nature of the business, purchasers are known by a variety of nomenclature: customer, consumer, client, patient, pupil or student, citizen, constituent, taxpayer, and internal customer. It becomes the role of marketing and sales to identify these various players and gather as much information about them and their buying habits as possible. In the online world of marketing, there are software tools for those purposes, such as Google Analytics, by which marketers can determine how many unique visitors there are on a website, how long they visited (i.e., the "stickiness" of the site), how many page views they made, and how often they returned. In general, there is a whole body of knowledge that has been developed, accompanied by numerous books and publications, on the topic of how to satisfy the customer. Many theories, concepts, and buzzwords have become popular, such as customer centricity, exceeding customer expectations, customer relations management (CRM), raving fans, the consumer is king, customer value-stream mapping, purchasing power, customer loyalty, and net-promoter score.

Clearly, from business strategy, marketing, and sales perspectives, customers must be satisfied so that they continue purchasing the products and services and become loyal customers of a particular company, such as the fans of Apple, Starbucks, and Tim Horton's, to name a few. In fact, Peter Drucker, the acknowledged dean and guru of management thinking, put it this way, "The purpose of a company is to create a customer...The only profit center is a customer." The critical question that must be asked by every business is, "Who are our real customers?" In marketing parlance, a business needs to determine its "target markets" and "targeted customers."

According to Excellence Canada's "Excellence, Innovation and Wellness Standard," every organization should:

- Clearly identify its customer target markets.
- Establish what its customers need, require, desire, want, and value.
- Create a customer experience plan that is linked to the strategic plan and includes tactics for maximizing customer satisfaction, retention, and loyalty.
- Determine the many points of contact with a customer and what the "moments of truth" are for a customer dealing with the business.
- Communicate regularly with its customers using a variety of contact methods such as meetings, focus groups, conferences, telephone, e-mail, text-messages, mail, social networking like Twitter or Facebook, blogs, newsletters, surveys, etc.
- Have a process in place for soliciting feedback from its customers using a variety of methods as above.
- Have a process that allows customers to give unsolicited input.
- Have a tracking system and a process for dealing with customer comments, complaints, compliments, and suggestions.
- Measure and manage customer-retention statistics, and analyse the causes of any losses and take action to address the root causes.
- Evaluate trends for meeting customer-service delivery standards and use the information for customer retention and continuous improvement of products, services, and the "customer experience."

Introductory marketing textbooks usually describe the marketing function using a model called the four P's of marketing:

1. Products: Related topics include branding, brand loyalty, product differentiation, design, quality, reliability, accuracy, warranty, expected useful life, product life cycles, service, innovation, obsolescence features, benefits, ease of use, bells and whistles.
2. Price: At what price should the business sell its products and services? Is it going to use a low-price strategy to sell large volumes at low margins, or will it sell higher-priced products or services/experiences where a higher price is part of the perception of quality? Examples of the latter include Walmart or Costco compared to The Bay or Nordstrom; Holiday Inn or Comfort Inn compared to The Ritz or the Four Seasons hotels; Jet Blue or Southwest Airlines compared to Lufthansa or Air Emirates; Denney's or Jack Astor's compared to The Keg or Morton's Steakhouse; Hyundai or Mazda or Honda vs. Mercedes or BMW or Audi; Acer or Lenovo vs. Apple or HP.
3. Place (Distribution): One example is the physical- vs. online-shopping location (Chapters / Indigo or Barnes and Noble [brick-and-mortar] vs. Amazon.com).
4. Promotion: Topics include advertising (via all media, including digital), public relations, publicity, online/Internet marketing, social-media sites (Facebook, Twitter, LinkedIn, YouTube, Pinterest, Snapchat, Instagram, etc.).

Another critical question for a business to ask is, "What does the customer really value?" In marketing terms, this is often referred to as the Unique Selling Proposition or USP of the business. A business or organization needs to find out from its customers what they really value, and the best way to find out is often simply to ask them. Companies conduct focus groups, one-on-one meetings, or phone interviews with key customers or potential customers. Often, third-party, market-research companies are engaged to do post-purchase customer surveys, especially for big-ticket items, such as cars. One such company is J.D. Powers.

Many companies employ "mystery shoppers" or have the boss go "undercover" at the business, to learn first-hand how the employees are treating customers.

Listening to what "purchasers" have to say (i.e., the voice of the customer) is critical for helping commercial businesses and other organizations with planning, to be discussed later.

Force Two: Purchasers

Summary

The more an enterprise knows about the Purchasers of its products and services, the better it will be able to meet and exceed their expectations. The Purchaser may not be the end-user of the products or services if the organization is very large and has a procurement department, such as in Governments and the military. Continuing to satisfy and exceed the needs and expectations of the "customer", who may be an internal or external customer, is paramount for the long-term success of every business and organization.

Action Items

1. Clearly identify who are the Purchasers of your products and services
2. Determine who are the customers and end-users
3. Ensure you know what your customers value, need, want and desire
4. Maximize customer satisfaction to achieve customer retention
5. Communicate regularly with your customers and listen to their feedback- the "voice of the customer"- so that you can enhance the customer experience and create customer loyalty.

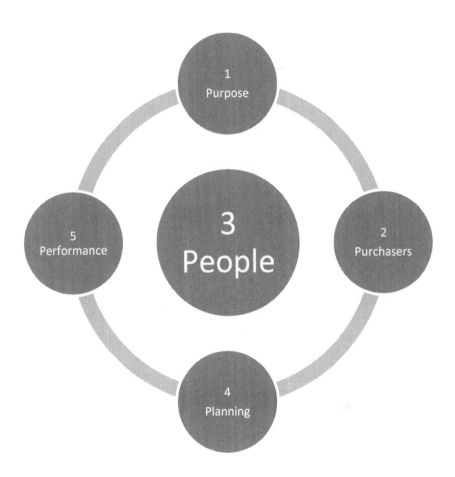

Chapter 3

Force Three: People

The expression, "people are our greatest asset," while hackneyed, is absolutely true. The people in an organization bring its purpose to life, execute its business plan, and carry out the various processes needed to serve the purchasers of the organization's products and services.

Even in our technological age in which people are connected around the world via the Internet; purchasers search, shop, and pay online; and fulfilment processes are increasingly automated; people are still required to ensure that the websites are up-to-date and inviting, that e-commerce functions smoothly, and that goods and services are delivered to the purchaser. People at Amazon.com are even conducting experiments to see whether flying drones(!) can be efficiently utilized to deliver parcels (loaded into plastic containers) to customers.

Multimillion-dollar businesses today can be run with few employees, but until such time as robots and artificial intelligence (AI) take over (which may not be that far into the future), people are still very much needed to run most organizations. In the future, though, there will be a greater need for people skilled in information processing and technology.

Consider economic history for a moment. Over many hundreds of years, our society has been transformed from one that is based in hunting and gathering into an agrarian-based society into a manufacturing culture involved in mass production. At that point, factory lines-of-production where people did the same repetitive task over and over again all day were developed, and managers implemented time-and-motion studies to increase worker productivity. This often resulted in sweatshops, intolerable working conditions, and the birth of the labour-union movement to protect the rights of the workers from the employers who had all the power and capital. With the rise of capitalism, workers were regarded as just another factor of production like raw materials, utilities, and money.

As machinery and equipment became more sophisticated and computerized, goods could be produced more quickly with better quality and fewer workers. And so the industrial economy was replaced by a service economy where more people worked in white-collar jobs (as opposed to industrial-age, blue-collar jobs) such as banking, the stock market, finance, insurance, import-export, government services at all levels, professional services such as law, accounting, engineering, and the medical professions, to name but a few. More people are now employed in office jobs than in factories or on farms.

And while the service economy hasn't gone away, more and more people are working in industries that can be regarded as high-tech, including software development, computing, mobile computing and applications (apps), and telecommunications. In short, we have entered the information age, and knowledge workers are most in demand. In fact, while a high-school diploma may have been more than enough education in the industrial age, and a bachelor's degree was all that was needed for a good job in the service age, a master's degree may become a prerequisite for a leadership position in the information age.

Some futurists contend that the information age will soon give way to the knowledge age, where people with highly specialized knowledge, as opposed to generalists, will be most in demand.

However, regardless of what sector a business is in— agriculture, mining, manufacturing, import/export, warehousing/distribution, transportation, communications, services, information, or knowledge—the essentials of business will always be the imperatives of attracting, recruiting, training, motivating, and retaining the best people for the available jobs.

As Jim Collins puts it in his book, *Good to Great,* businesses need to have the right people sitting in the right seat on the right bus going in the right direction.

When discussing the importance of people, it is useful to look at the people who fulfil one or more of the following roles:

1. Leaders
2. Managers
3. Individuals
4. Teams (made up of people from the three categories above)
5. Partners, Suppliers, Strategic Alliances, and Professionals

Leaders

There have been more books and articles written on leadership than on any other business topic. Many people who have been acknowledged as successful leaders or innovators in business, government, academics, or politics, have written books detailing their respective leadership styles and success principles. See the Appendix B for a listing of some of these books.

The numerous models or styles of leadership include:

- Action-Centered Leadership
- Adaptive Leadership
- Authentic Leadership
- Crisis Leadership
- Dynamic Leadership
- Effective Organizational Leadership
- Emotional Intelligence
- Growing Leaders
- Inspirational Leadership
- Leadership and Decision Making
- Leadership Best Practices
- Leadership by Example
- Leadership Excellence
- Leadership IQ
- Leadership versus Management
- Leadership, Influence and Trust

- Leading Under Pressure
- Liberating Leadership
- Military Leadership
- Principle Centred Leadership
- Servant Leadership
- Situational Leadership
- Situational Leadership
- The Art of Leadership
- The Leadership Challenge
- Traditional Leadership
- Transactional/Transformational Leadership
- Transformational Leadership

There are also numerous leadership assessment tools and instruments, and leadership development and training programs, including:

- 360 Degree Assessments
- DISC
- Leadership Effectiveness and Adaptability Description (LEAD)
- Life Styles Inventory (LSI)
- Management Effectiveness Profile Survey (MEPS)
- The Leadership Practices Inventory (LPI)
- True Colours

Highly successful leaders have personal styles that they integrate with those of their team members. Regardless of the models or theories of leadership that are used, leadership is vital in every organization and at all levels of the organization, not only in the C-suite.

Every business must have effective leaders at each level of the organization if it is to remain successful in today's marketplace. And the characteristics of effective leaders can be learned through the large body of available research on the topic. Opinions differ on who can become an effective leader. Some people are of the opinion that leaders are born, not made. Others agree with the late Green Bay Packers coach Vince Lombardi, who said, "Contrary to the opinion of many people, leaders are not born. Leaders are made, and they are made by effort and hard work."

Leaders need to be able to set the mission and direction of the organization. They need to be forward-looking and create a compelling vision of the future while still being situated firmly in the present and cognizant of the organization's past.

Leaders need to be honest and have integrity if they are going to be believed and trusted. They should be inspiring, competent, fair-minded, supportive, self-controlled, and broad-minded.

Essentially, leadership comes from ordinary people who care enough to get extraordinary things doing in their organization. Basic initiatives of the leader include:

- Promoting new ideas
- Gaining better results
- Striving to implement a policy
- Living a philosophy
- Gaining the full engagement of people within an organization
- "Leadership is communicating to people their worth and potential so clearly that they come to

see it in themselves" (Stephen Covey, *Seven Habits of Highly Effective People*).

- Leadership is about ordinary people who care enough to get extraordinary things done in their organization.

Managers

The second group of people who play a vital role in organizations are managers. Leaders and managers are interrelated, but they have their own purposes and actions. While managers are often also leaders, their day-to-day role is distinct when they are performing management functions. Following are some ways to describe the difference between leaders and managers.

Management focuses upon dealing with the organization by developing plans and budgets, organizing and staffing, and directing and managing performance. The manager focuses on the need to "do things right."

Leadership focuses upon dealing with change by determining where the organization is going and what it will do, bringing people with vision on board, and energizing and inspiring. The leader focuses on the need to "do the right things."

Put another way, leadership is dynamic; it is about change and moving the status quo. Management is about perfecting what already exists. If leaders are the architects, then managers are the builders. Leadership requires the ability to determine a direction for the organization, translate the vision and big picture into smaller tasks, bring others on board who will commit to the organization's vision and tasks, and energize people to accomplish the tasks. The leaders of the organization are found at every level of the company where they carry out the same leadership duties in leading their department or team. They clearly communicate the vision so that people do understand and support it. The credibility of the leader is very important. Leaders focus upon equipping their teams with everything they need in order to do the work. This includes skill development, knowledge, coaching, resource support, feedback, a helping hand, and recognition. Leaders are able to assess their own strengths and weaknesses, and work to improve their leadership practices through lifelong learning

Achieving the task

Developing individual

Building the team

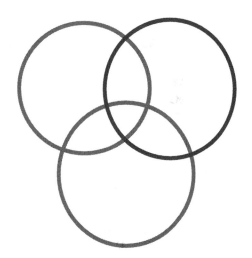

According to John Adair, a British writer on leadership, the leader is responsible for three main areas as shown in the Venn diagram. He emphasizes that these areas overlap and when in balance, the leader achieves maximum effectiveness.

Managers are responsible for:

- Hiring
- Training
- Communicating
- Planning
- Organizing

- Delegating
- Motivating

As a manager, you control things: money, costs, information, systems, inventory, facilities, resources, tools, and time. But you don't manage people. You lead or empower people; you implement and motivate.

The key difference between management and leadership is that leadership is dynamic, it is about change, and it is about moving the status quo, while management is about perfecting what the company already has.

> "Leadership is about coping with change…Management is about coping with complexity" (John Kotter).
>
> "Leaders are the architects…Managers are the builders" (John Marriotti).
>
> "Leadership focuses on the creation of a common vision…Management is the design of work…it's about controlling" (George Weathersby).

To build a successful organization, there need to be various people playing different roles in order for things to run smoothly. Some of these roles are easily defined while others may have confusing boundaries, such as the difference between a manager and a leader. You can be a manager and a leader at the same time, but just because you're a phenomenal leader doesn't guarantee you'll be a great manager, and vice-versa. Drucker wrote that managers accept the status quo and are more like soldiers in the military. They know that orders and plans are crucial, and their job is to keep their vision on the company's current goals.

Often one individual acts both as a leader and a manager in a business or organization. The key to knowing how to act and when to do so is figuring out what is required to effect positive change. If new goals or a new vision are required, then it is time to act as a leader. If staying focused on and executing the existing goals or vision are required, then it is important to act as a manager. Clearly, both leadership and management are critically important.

Here are twenty distinctions between a manager and a leader:

1. A manager has a short-range perspective. A leader has a long-range perspective.
2. A manager plans how and when. A leader asks what and why.
3. A manager eyes the bottom line. A leader eyes the horizon.
4. A manager imitates others. A leader originates.
5. A manager accepts the status quo. A leader challenges the status quo.
6. A manager does things correctly. A leader does the correct thing.
7. A manager seeks continuity. A leader seeks change.
8. A manager focuses on goals for improvement. A leader focuses on goals of innovation.
9. A manager bases power on position or authority. A leader bases power on personal influence.
10. A manager demonstrates skill in technical competence. A leader demonstrates skill in selling the vision.
11. A manager demonstrates skill in administration. A leader demonstrates skill in dealing with ambiguity.

12. A manager demonstrates skill in supervision. A leader demonstrates skill in persuasion.
13. A manager works toward employee compliance. A leader works toward employee commitment.
14. A manager plans tactics. A leader plans strategy.
15. A manager sets standard operating procedures. A leader sets policy.
16. A manager is risk averse. A leader takes the necessary risks.
17. A manager uses a "transactional" communication style. A leader uses a "transformational" communication style.
18. A manager builds success through maintenance of quality. A leader builds success through employee commitment.
19. A manager plans, budgets, and designs detail steps. A leader develops vision and the strategies to achieve it.
20. A manager sets standards of performance. A leader sets standards of excellence.

Teams

Unless a business consists of a one-man or one-woman band—a sole proprietorship with no other employees—people generally have co-workers with whom they form a group or a team. There is an important difference between the two. A group of people do not necessarily share common goals and objectives, nor do they necessarily share a common vision or values. (See chapter 1, "Force One: Purpose.") Groups of people may work for the same organization and department, but that does not mean that they are working together as a team. They are often working in "silos" and do not interact with or rely on one another.

For a group to become a true team, the co-workers involved need shared goals, leadership, participation, common organization and processes, clear roles, and a team focus rather than a personal focus. Teams consist of two or more people with a common vision, mission, and goals, who rely on one another for success. All teams in sports fit this description.. And, of course, essential components of any sports team are its coaches and trainers. It is a coach's responsibility to ensure that the players do, in fact, play as a team and complement one another. Often the most talented players do not work best as team players, and so the coach has to take into account interpersonal relationships, chemistry, and whether teammates like and respect one another.

All teams in sports fit this description. A perfect illustration of a team working in unison for a single goal is a rowing team, in which eight men and/or women are completely in sync, stroking their oars in the water to the timing called out by the coxswain. If just one rower is out of sync or gets what is called "a crab," it throws the whole boat off stride, slows it down, and can even result in the boat losing the race.

In an organization, teams are often organized functionally (e.g., the marketing department, the sales team, the production team, etc.). Often, especially in large and multinational companies, team members may work virtually with others who may be located in various parts of the world, coordinate with team members in different time zones, and report to managers who may be based in another country. With the Internet and related technologies such as videoconferencing, Skype, Apple's FaceTime, and virtual-meeting or chat software such as Adobe or WebEx, it is very easy for team members to work together without having to leave their offices. They just have to avoid setting meeting times that may fall in the middle of the night for some team members.

For many projects, cross-functional teams are formed that require the knowledge and skills of team members from different functional departments, depending on the nature of the project or assignment. A team may be comprised of people from, for example, production, marketing, sales, finance, IT, and logistics.

However, just because people have been assigned to work as a team, does not mean that they will form a high-performing team. This is where team-building comes in. There are numerous team-building training programs that teach team members to rely on and trust one another and to work together to overcome obstacles. Some of these are outdoor retreats in which team members have to overcome physical challenges such as rope-climbing or obstacle courses, and need the help and encouragement of their fellow team members.   There are many reality-TV shows such as *Survivor* where players are assigned to a team, and have to work with that team to avoid being "voted off the island." The only problem with such reality shows is that participants are really working to win and, accordingly, will often intentionally sabotage fellow team members whom they perceive as competitors for the top prize.

Building a cohesive senior leadership team is a critical role for a CEO as it is for any leader and manager. There are literally hundreds of books and articles and courses on the dynamics of team building. However, there is a body of knowledge and best practices of what makes a well-functioning team.

Team-building is important because one of the critical areas for success in today's fast-paced marketplace is the ability for everyone in the organization to work together effectively and in support of each other. The goals of providing high-quality products and excellent customer service require that organizations foster a supportive, team-based approach.

Many elements need to be present in order for a group of people to form an effective team and stay focused to achieve collective goals. Individuals already possess a wealth of strengths, skills, and team-oriented personality traits; successful team-building depends on the willingness of the members to tap into their gifts.

Again, all teams are groups, but not all groups are teams. In today's world, groups are formed for many reasons such as to manufacture items, solve problems, organize events, play games, present issues, learn things, and govern. These working groups can be quite successful in their efforts but may never become a team. Groups become a team when they exhibit certain characteristics and relationships.

According to Bruce Tuckman, a group-dynamics theorist, new teams usually go through five distinct and observable stages:

1. Forming: The team is formed.
2. Storming: Often there is disagreement and lack of progress, even negative productivity, until stage 3 happens.
3. Norming: The team develops rules, codes of conduct, and norms for how they will work together.
4. Performing: Great progress is made, and the team starts to perform at a very high level.
5. Adjourning: The project or work of the team is done, and the team disbands.

Whenever people are brought together as a team, they will move naturally through the above stages before they turn into a well-focused and performing unit. All teams will follow this process and pass through each stage. This process will happen whenever there are changes in the makeup of an existing team.

It is crucial for leaders of teams to be able to recognize the stage that their teams are in and assist them to address and resolve all issues and concerns, so that they are able to progress and achieve their goals.

Team Behaviours and Roles. The regular use of positive, interpersonal and team behaviours is one of the features of a team that makes it different from a group. The use of these behaviours brings the team four important benefits.

1. Members work with one another in an open, easy way.
2. Ideas and opinions are exchanged in an honest, considerate manner.
3. Trust and "good feelings about the team" grow in the positive climate.
4. Team decisions are supported as all members are involved in process.

Ground Rules. Effective teams use the behaviours to set standards or norms to guide the way they go about achieving the team goal (the "what") and the way they interact (the "how"). This list of expectations is often referred to as the team's ground rules, the regular use of which promotes positive, open, and supportive communication among team members, which fosters teamwork.

The following are some important ground rules used by effective teams to guide their process or interactions.

- Time is organized and used well.
- All members join in all team activities.
- All information is shared.
- Discussions are focused.
- Difficulties with team members are discussed openly.
- Consensus is used to make decisions.
- Distractions are not condoned.

- Statements/ideas are questioned, examined, disagreed with, commented upon, given with explanations or reasons or examples.

Important Interpersonal Behaviours. Team members display a willingness to make sure that teamwork happens. These are some of the most important actions they take:

- Looking at the speaker, nodding, and paraphrasing to show understanding.
- Helping members to enter discussion, and discouraging constant talkers.
- Offering ideas, information, facts, opinions, and values.
- Asking questions to clarify, probe, prove, test, or get more information.
- Discussing difficulties with team members openly.
- Speaking up to support, recognize, praise, and expand ideas.
- Listening actively and then stating concerns, or disagreeing and giving reasons.
- Recognizing there is conflict and then listening to help clarify and resolve it.
- Helping members to see similar views or to reconcile their differences.
- Reviewing ideas/points/actions to indicate what has been done to date.
- Reminding/praising the group about using ground rules.

- Organizing team sessions to meet team needs and use time well.

Individuals

Clearly, leaders, managers, and teams are comprised of individuals. The individual person is the essential building block for all the strengths of not only the People force but indeed of all Big Five Forces. Without good people nothing happens.

As Jim Collins puts it in his best-selling book *Good to Great*, you need the right people in the right seats on the right bus going in the right direction.

A business needs people who have the right skills, knowledge, experience, expertise, and, probably most important of all, the right attitude. Employers should "hire for attitude and train for skill," as the saying goes.

Without qualified and capable individuals who are passionate about what they do, an organization cannot hope to satisfy the purchasers of its products and services and deliver the peak performance that the organization is capable of achieving.

The Human Resources (HR) or "people department" of an organization plays a critical role in helping an organization to attract, recruit, train, motivate, compensate, and retain the best people for each position.

There are several tried and tested methodologies for hiring the right people, including the popular "Behavioural-Based Interviewing" in which an interviewer asks a candidate, "Tell me about a time when…" the candidate had to deal with a problem, make a tough decision, and so forth, because the candidate's past experience may be a predictor of future performance at the new hiring organization.

Several instruments and assessments are designed to get the best candidate-fit for a particular position. Assessment tools include IQ Tests, EQ tests, behavioural tests, Myers-Briggs, True Colours, and DISC, to name but a few.

The DISC assessment tool assesses four character traits: dominance, influence, steadiness, and compliance. A candidate answers a series of twenty-four, multiple-choice questions. Based on the candidate's responses, a computer program generates a DISC profile that shows which of the four traits are relatively high and which are relatively low for that candidate. There are thousands of sample profiles in the DISC database, and they show ideal profiles for certain types of jobs, such as CEO, Sales, Accounting, IT, and Administration.

For example, you would expect salespeople to be influential or have a "high I" as well as driven or have a "high D." A CEO usually has a "high D," a higher "I," but a "low S," which means that he or she has low steadiness and is easily bored by the status quo. CEOs also have low compliance or "low C's." Often their C's are just below the zero line, showing that they sometimes tend to break policies and procedures— even those that they helped to create. For accounting jobs and other jobs that require accuracy and repetition, you would expect individuals to be steady and policy-compliant, that is, they would have a "high S's" and "High C's" in their profiles.

Human Resources, Healthy Workplace and Mental Health@Work. When thinking about People, you also need to consider 1) whether the organization is a Healthy Workplace, and 2) the psychological health and safety of the workplace as established by the Mental Health Commission of Canada. As stated in the Excellence, Innovation, and Wellness (EIW) Standard of Excellence Canada, "leaders need to actively promote a culture of work/life balance." Furthermore, "there needs to be a policy (or policies) that clearly demonstrate a commitment to people and wellness includes the elements of: physical environment and occupational health and safety; health and lifestyle practices; workplace culture and supportive environment; and mental health. Healthy employees with a good work-life balance are more likely to stay, are more productive, and contribute to the long-term success of the organization. Policies could address such things as mental health (including workload issues), flexible work arrangements where feasible, physical health, and safety."

Of course, the organization also needs to have human-resources policies that address relevant human-rights legislation and issues to protect against harassment and discrimination in the workplace. According to Excellence Canada's Standard, organizations with several employees should have a Strategic Human Resources Plan, and a Wellness Plan that links to the overall Strategic Plan.

- Human resource planning identifies the skills and capabilities needed to achieve the broad objectives in the strategic plan. (See chapter 4, "Force Four: Planning.")
- A typical Human Resources Plan would include strategies for recruitment, retention, succession planning, capacity building, organizational development and training, compensation and benefits, union relations (if applicable), and rewards and recognition.
- A typical Wellness Plan would address the needs of employees and strategies to address physical environment and occupational health and safety, health and lifestyle practices, workplace culture, and supportive environment and mental health.
- A typical "Voice of the Employee" strategy would include collection of data for employee engagement and satisfaction.
- Key indicators that these plans link to the overall Strategic Plan include:
    o Employee engagement and satisfaction.
    o Productivity measures.
    o Absenteeism rates.
    o Short- and long-term disability rates.
    o Return to work statistics.

- o Accident/injury rates.
- o Grievances and/or complaints.
- o Any lawsuits.
- o Turnover/retention rates.
- o Extended health-benefits utilization.
- o Employee Assistance Plan (EAP) usage.
- o Involvement in wellness programs.
- o Involvement in Corporate Social Responsibility (CSR) initiatives (volunteer hours, funds raised, etc.).
- In addition, organizations need a system in place for recruitment, selection, and on-boarding of employees.
- Employees need to understand their roles and responsibilities as outlined in current job descriptions.
- There also needs to be a system in place for management of employee performance. (See chapter 5, "Force Five: Performance.") Performance-management approaches provide objective feedback to people on how they are doing. It also helps to identify areas where education and/or training would provide opportunities for individual growth and advancement. Performance management reviews can include:
  - o Performance against identified goals and objectives.
  - o Job-description review.
  - o Career expectations.
  - o Development and learning needs.
  - o Support for ethical behaviour and organizational values.
- Improving leadership, management, and supervisory interpersonal skills and abilities is a high priority, and there should be a leadership-development program in place to improve the interpersonal skills and abilities for managing employees.

- Employees should be able to seek assistance in addressing issues, concerns, and opportunities.
- Whenever possible, employees should be involved in decisions that directly impact them such as working on process-improvement teams, participation in evaluating new products and services, evaluation of new partners and suppliers, and wellness programs.
- Innovative ideas should be encouraged, shared, and celebrated.

Partners, Suppliers, Strategic Alliances, and Professionals

Other key people for an organization include partners, suppliers, strategic allies, and professional support. No business or organization can function effectively without strong relationships with several partners, suppliers, and alliances.

Partners may be classified as financial or nonfinancial. Financial partners may get profit sharing, commissions, royalties, referral fees, and the like. Nonfinancial partners may include volunteers, charities, and agencies that may promote one another. Roles, responsibilities, and rewards of the partners need to be clearly identified and agreed upon. So do the partnership goals and objectives. Having trusted relationship with partners and suppliers is obviously essential.

Often partners and suppliers are involved in the strategic planning of the business and may be involved in product innovation and development. For example, Cargill Value-Added Meats is very involved with its main customer, McDonald's, in not only the quality of the chicken they supply, but also in product innovation such as chicken snack wraps,

McNuggets, and so forth. Software or application developers are closely involved with hardware and smartphone manufacturers. Microsoft, for example, arranged to have its Windows software installed on most PCs. Google has supplied at no charge its Android operating system to Samsung and many other smartphone manufacturers.

There need to be performance measures and feedback and evaluation mechanisms in place to gauge performance and identify any issues among partners. The criteria that relate to suppliers (see below) could also serve as a checklist for satisfaction levels in this category as well.

In formal contracts and agreements, partners need to agree upon terms regarding the following:

- Training
- On-boarding
- Governance
- Conflict resolution
- Corrective action
- Improvement initiatives
- Correspondence
- Performance-review meetings
- Notice provisions
- Termination clauses
- Arbitration procedures in the event of a dispute
- Legal jurisdiction for any legal action

A partnership or alliance should be a win-win-win proposition, that is, both parties as well as the customer win.

Suppliers. Many businesses exist to supply you with the goods and/or services—"inputs"—that you need to operate your business. These inputs may be raw materials needed for manufacturing, semifinished goods that require your processing, or finished goods that your business wholesales or retails. Selection of suppliers may involve policies for procurement, such as proposals, tenders, RFPs, RFQs, and approved vendor lists. Before committing to a supplier, it is a good practice to check references from its other customers to find out about its track record, references from banks and credit bureaus to learn about its credit worthiness, records in better business and consumer agencies, and, depending on the nature of the services to be provided, records, if any, with the police.

The key to selecting suppliers is to consider the performance standards that suppliers are expected to meet, such as the following:

- Quality of goods and services
- Consistency
- Price
- On-budget
- Just-in-time delivery
- On-time delivery
- Accuracy
- Service
- Reliability
- Relevance
- Value for money
- Cost-effectiveness
- Research and Development
- Innovation

Policies should be in place for the release or termination of suppliers who are not performing according to established, agreed-upon standards. All the conflict resolution and dispute resolution/arbitration mechanisms that are recommended for partners may apply equally to suppliers.

Professionals. Businesses also depend on the expertise of many professionals and consultants who play an integral role in the success of the business. Professionals and consultants include:

- Lawyers
- Accountants
- Auditors
- Engineers
- Architects
- Interior designers
- Real-estate professionals
- Appraisers
- Insurance agents
- Commercial banks
- Investment banks
- Merchant banks
- Stock brokers
- Financial advisors
- Financial planners
- Business brokers
- Franchise consultants
- Business consultants in a variety of specialties
- Performance-management consultants
- Back-office process providers

Force Three: People

Summary

To sum up the People Force, the following are the critical players in an organization:

- Leaders (including executives, the C-suite, and senior management)
- Managers (line and staff or function managers and supervisors)
- Individuals (frontline employees)
- Teams (made up of people from the three categories above)
- Partners, suppliers, strategic alliances and professionals

All of the above people are critical to the success of the business. Clearly, the People Force is a critical success factor (CSF) for every business and organization.

Action Items

1. Attract, hire, train and retain the best **People** who will help make your business or organization very successful
2. Ensure that you have effective leaders as they are critical for setting the strategic direction and the "tone-at-the-top"
3. Ensure that your managers are competent as they are ultimately responsible for executing the business plan and achieving the goals
4. Ensure that there is a direct line-of-site from the desk of the CEO/President to the individual employees on the front line who are carrying out the mission of the business and serving customers, so that everyone

knows what is important and how they contribute to the success of the business

5. Encourage and enable team-work, communicate constantly, motivate and inspire, recognize and reward good performance, and a create a Healthy Workplace ® culture in which people are engaged and enjoy going to work and feel that they are contributing to the success of the organization.

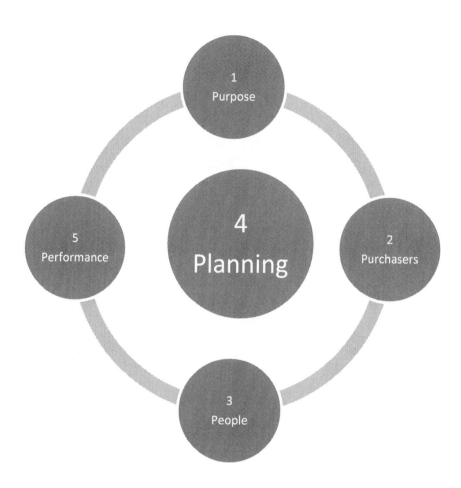

Chapter 4

Force Four: Planning

Let's recap what we have discussed so far. We have looked at the purpose of the business, the purchasers of the products and services, and the people involved in the organization. The next of the Big Five Forces is Planning.

The reason that planning is so critical can be summed up in the following quote from Lewis Carroll's book, *Alice's Adventures in Wonderland*.

"Cheshire Cat, would you tell me please, which way I ought to go from here?" asked Alice.

"That depends a good deal on where you want to get to," replied the cat.

Or, to reiterate, if you don't know where you are going, any road will get you there.

Clearly a business or organization needs to know where it would like to go in the future, so that all of its resources (money, assets, and the expertise, skills, time, and effort of its personnel) can be utilized most effectively and efficiently.

When discussing the Planning Force, there are different time-horizons and levels to consider. The overarching, long-range plan for the organization is called the "strategic plan." It sets out the plans, goals, objectives, and actions for the organization for the next three to ten years.

Strategic Planning

The following are some of the key elements of strategic planning:

The first decision is the selection of a cross-functional team who will be doing the strategic planning. This should not be limited to the board of directors and C-suite executives; it should include senior and middle management, supervisors, frontline employees, customers, suppliers, partners, strategic alliances, professional advisors, shareholders, and other stakeholders. (See chapter 3, "Force Three: People.") The people doing the strategic planning must have a strong understanding of the organization and its business and customers, because there is no substitute for experience when developing a strategic plan. Furthermore, the strategic-planning team must be open to feedback from all stakeholders when developing the plan.

The next requirement is the selection of a model or framework or road map for strategic planning, such as this Big Five Forces model. (Other models that may be used include Excellence Canada's "Excellence, Innovation and Wellness" standard, framework and criteria:, the Blue Ocean Strategy of Kim and Mauborgne; Peter Drucker's *The Five Most Important Questions You Need to Ask*; various planning models outlined in *Strategy Safari* by Mintzberg, Ahlstrand, and Lampel; Michael Porter's *Competitive Strategy*; Norton and Kaplan's *Balanced Scorecard*, and numerous other strategic-planning frameworks. Regardless of which model is selected for doing the strategic planning, they all have common elements and goals, even though they may start at different points.

An organization must be willing to dedicate time, resources, and energy to the process of developing a strategic plan; there are no shortcuts. As the business environment changes, so too must the strategic plan.

One straightforward and logical approach to strategic planning is to answer these five questions and follow the related steps:

1. Where are we now?

2. Where do we want to be?

3. What do we have to do to get there?

4. How do we do it?

5. What actions do we need to take to get there?

1. Where are we now? Most strategic plans will include a review and in-depth analysis of the following:

- Mission, Vision, Values (See chapter 1, "Force One: Purpose.")
- Customer identification (See chapter 2, "Force Two: Purchasers.")
- Clarity around the organization's value proposition and Unique Selling Proposition (USP)
- The organization's Strengths, Weaknesses, Opportunities, and Threats, commonly known as a SWOT analysis. The organization must examine its internal capabilities as well as scan external factors—often referred to by the acronym PESTLE (Political, Economic, Social, Tax, Legal, and Environmental)—over which the organization usually has little control.

  When doing the SWOT analysis it is useful to answer the following general questions:

- What business are we really in?
- What was the original vision of our organization?
- How has this vision changed?
- How have we changed?
- Who are our customers and stakeholders?
- What are our customers' needs?
- What are our customers' expectations?
- What principal products and services do we provide?
- What are our strengths, weaknesses, opportunities and threats (SWOT)?
- What values and principles do we adhere to that must guide our decisions?
- What is our corporate philosophy?
- What policy decisions must we make?

Strengths and weaknesses refer to factors that are internal to the organization that are working for or against the organization. Depending on the answer to the questions below, a given factor may either be a strength or a weakness. If the answer is favourable to the organization, it can be considered a strength; if it is unfavourable, it is a weakness. In examining strengths and weaknesses, the team should ask the following questions:

- How loyal are our customers?
- How quickly can we respond to the changing needs of our customers?
- How is our market share trending?
- What is our financial situation, including cash position and working capital?
- What is our fixed overhead and costs?
- What are our variable costs?
- How much is our payroll costing every month?

- How productive and engaged are our employees?
- How skilled is our workforce?
- Does our corporate culture support our mission?
- How up-to-date is our technology, both hardware and software?
- Do we face any technological constraints?
- Have we got an effective website and e-commerce capability?
- Are we utilizing social-media tools such as Facebook, Twitter, and LinkedIn?

Opportunities and threats are those factors outside the organization that are influencing its effectiveness. Again, any given factor may be an opportunity or a threat depending on whether it has a positive or negative influence on the organization. In examining opportunities and threats, it will be useful to ask the following questions:

- Are new competitors entering our marketplace?
- What strategy changes are our competitors making?
- Are we entering new markets?
- What changes are driving the economy?
- What technological changes are affecting our business?
- Are we facing any constraints with our inputs and resources?
- Are we able to respond to labour force trends?
- What actions are required to implement these policies?
- What are our priorities and what resources do we need?

When the team examines the possible threats facing the organization, it is also useful to consider an article that Michael Watkins and Max Bazerman wrote in the *Harvard Business Review*, entitled: "Predictable Surprises: The Disasters You Should Have Seen Coming."

The title, of course, appears to be an oxymoron; if something is a surprise, how can it have been predictable? But Watkins and Bazerman argue that, although the exact timing and specifics of the threat, may not have been foreseen, the fact that the threat was a real possibility should nevertheless have been predicted and planned for.

Many disasters, when analysed with the knowledge of hindsight, should have been predictable, such as:

- The 9/11 terror attacks on the Twin Towers in New York City
- The Hurricane Katrina disaster in New Orleans
- The corporate frauds and scandals of Enron, WorldCom, Adelphi, Hollinger, Livent, Parmalat, and Bernie Madoff's Ponzi scheme

It can be argued that there were plenty of warning signs about all of the above threats, but that governments and regulators, businesses, and individuals failed to recognize the threats, prioritize them, and mobilize the resources to prevent them.

2. Where do we want to be? The ability to answer that question requires a long-term vision for the business. This has been discussed under "Purpose" so it won't be reviewed in this section. However, the owners and senior management must have a vision for where they would like to take their business in the long run. What will the organization look like in, say, ten, fifteen, or twenty years?

It is useful for the planning team to create a BHAG, which stands for "Big, Hairy, Audacious Goal." This is a goal that is so big that it is almost outrageous, but it is something that the business can strive for even if the chance of realizing it is very remote. Jim Collins, in his book *Good to Great*, gives the example of the time when he challenged Starbucks founder Howard Shultz and his team to come up with a BHAG. Initially they came to the table with the number of Starbucks coffee shops that they would have in a ten-year period. But Collins called that goal "business in the usual course of growth" and challenged the team to come up with a more compelling BHAG.

When the team members came back for a follow-up planning session, they unveiled their new BHAG: "To become the most recognizable brand in the world." Collins agreed that this was, indeed, a BHAG, because the most recognizable brand in the world is Coca-Cola or Coke. But having this big, hairy, audacious goal changed how Starbucks viewed its business. It was no longer just enough to open many more thousand coffee shops; if Starbucks were to realize the dream of being the most recognizable brand in the world, it would need to make its coffee available in places other than just its coffee shops. Thus began the strategy of making Starbucks-branded coffee available in such other locations as hotel rooms, airplanes, restaurants, and supermarkets.

So having a BHAG is useful for creating a compelling vision.

3. What do we have to do to get there? This involves crafting a plan. The steps are outlined in the mnemonic, "GO TEAM."

Goals

Objectives

Targets

Evaluation

Activities

Measurement

Goals are the few, key, big-picture, broad, long-term plans that an organization is striving to achieve in the period covered by the strategic plan. As part of the strategic-planning process, the team should agree on what those few critical goals are. There should not be more than three to five main goals, so that the organization's resources don't become spread too thin and the team does not lose its laser-level focus. The goals should commit the people in the organization to specific courses of action. The plan will state how the goals are to be accomplished, that is, what concrete strategies and tactics must be undertaken to do so.

Examples of goals may be:

- Increase revenues and/or profits by A percent within B years.
- Increase customer satisfaction rates by C percent within D years.
- Reduce employee turnover by E percent within F years.
- Introduce three new products in the next two years.

- Expand the business into a new market by a realistic date.

Goals should also be SMART, which stands for:

- **S**pecific
- **M**easurable
- **A**chievable
- **R**esults-focused
- **T**ime-based

- *Specific.* If goals are not specific they just become general "wish lists." For example, if a personal goal is simply "to lose weight," it is too vague to be meaningful or motivational. But losing, say, ten pounds, is a specific (and measurable) goal, and the person will know when it has been achieved. Similarly, saying that your business goal is "to make more money" lacks specificity; one dollar more would achieve that goal. But if your goal is to increase profits by X percent or by Y dollars, then it is very clear to everyone what success looks like, and whether the goal has been realized can be objectively determined.
- *Measurable.* As shown above, if the goal is not measurable (e.g., in dollars or percentage or weight), then it will be difficult to know if it has been achieved. Measurement is critical when the "on-time" and "on-budget" considerations are present. Of course, measurement does not come into play with regard to goals that are of the yes-or-no type. For example, if the goal is to open up a new office in New York City or

launch two new products, it is either achieved or it isn't. But budget or time or profitability goals, for example, can be measured.

- *Achievable.* There is no point in setting a goal, even if it is specific and measurable, if it is not achievable; such a goal is meaningless and demotivating. For example, if you weigh two hundred pounds (but you should weigh about 180 pounds) and you decide that you want to lose fifty pounds, you may be endangering your health. But if your goal is to lose twenty pounds with a specific action plan of engaging a dietician to make sure you eat healthy foods in the right food groups and portions, and having a personal trainer develop an exercise program that you commit to several times a week, then losing twenty pounds should be achievable. If your business goal is to open offices in twelve new cities in the next year, but you do not have the human or financial resources to grow that much that quickly, then your goal is not achievable. It would need to be adjusted tosay, one new office per quarter, assuming that it was realistic to do so.

- *Results-focused.* This means that the goal results in meeting the objective that has been set. For example, if you wish to lose weight in order to look great for your daughter's wedding or to prepare before surgery, then the goal is results-focused. However, if your weight-loss goal is just the result of a New Year's resolution with no reason in mind, it is unlikely to be realized. Health clubs are typically busy in January, that is, after the New Year, but by February the number of people using health clubs drops dramatically. Similarly, if a business goal is to increase profits by doubling sales of one of the business's most profitable product lines, but doing so would mean dropping the price of the product too drastically, then the main objective of increasing revenue would probably not be achieved.

- *Time-based.* A goal has to have a deadline or period in which it is to be achieved; it cannot be open-ended and remain a meaningful goal. In the weight-loss example, if you said that with the help of the dietician and personal trainer and maybe support of family and friends, you planned to lose twenty pounds in the next eight months, your goal would be time-based.

When people know exactly what they want to achieve, and how, why, and by when, their goals are far more likely to be realized. Goals are dreams with deadlines. And SMART goals that have been developed by a team that has had input into their development, are also more likely to be achieved.

However, goals that are SMART are not necessarily the right goals for a business or organization. The senior leadership team needs to assess whether the goals that they have agreed upon for the next three to five years are the best goals, given the organization's resources and capabilities, mission, and vision (see chapter 1, "Force One: Purpose.")

Suppose an organization had the resources to achieve, not three to five goals, but just one. What should that one goal be? Let it be an overarching, "wildly important goal," or WIG.

One can think of many examples. At a community swimming pool, the WIG may be "safety in the pool at all times." For a police force, it may be "safety in the community." For a business, it may be "ensuring that there is enough capital to get the business off the ground until cash flow becomes positive." For a publicly traded company, it may be "maximizing shareholder value." For a government, it may be "balancing the budget and reducing the deficit." In essence, the WIG is the one goal that overrides all other goals and is most closely aligned to the mission of the organization.

Objectives are more specific and measureable than the broad goals above, and describe what the outcome will be as a result of the organization achieving the stated goals. For example, "The objective of achieving goal 1 will be to grow the business sufficiently to make an initial public offering (IPO) a possibility." Objectives must respond to the organization's strengths, weaknesses, opportunities, and strengths. Objectives convert the overarching strategic-mission statement (see chapter 1, "Force One: Purpose") into more specific performance outcomes.

Once these goals have been set, the next step is to set objectives for each of the goals. For example, if your business goal is to increase the number of your B-to-B customers, you may establish the following objectives:

- Increase the number of B-to-B customers by 10 percent, from 200 to 220.
- Retain 95 percent of the existing customers, that is, don't lose more than ten existing customers.
- Increase the average sales volume with B-to-B customers by 7 percent.
- Increase average gross margins by 2 percent.

In order to achieve the above objectives, the business should identify Critical Success Factors (CSFs), also known as Key Success Factors (KSFs), for each. In the example above, the CSFs may include:

- Hiring and training a team of professional account managers/sales people
- Hiring and training a team of dedicated customer-service representatives to follow-up with customers
- Incentivising the sales and customer-service teams when acquisition and retention objectives have been reached or exceeded

It is also useful up front to identify any Critical Obstacles and Barriers (COBs) to the CSFs that would affect the successful attainment of the objectives, so that such barriers can be prevented, resolved, or at least mitigated as soon as possible. In the above example, critical obstacles and barriers may be:

- High turnover of account representatives and/or customer-service representatives
- Ineffective on-boarding processes and training programs
- Lack of budget to offer competitive remuneration and incentives to attract and retain the team

Targets break down each goal into measurable milestones that need to be reached and completed within specified time frames if the goal is to be accomplished. A one-year goal may have quarterly or monthly targets, while a five-year goal will have annual targets, and so on.

Once all of this has been done, it is finally time to develop targets and tactics that will serve to mobilize the organization's people and resources to achieving the goals and objectives. Using the example above, these strategies and tactics may be:

- Develop a budget and secure the funding needed to achieve strategies below.
- Hire four new account representatives (ARs).
- Hire three new customer-service representatives (CSRs).
- Set up a dedicated sales and customer-service training department, and hire an experienced training manager.
- Train all new hires above as well as all the existing ARs and CSRs.

Evaluation means that at each of the target milestones, the team needs to evaluate whether the goal is being accomplished on time and on budget according to the plan that was laid out. And if it is not, then the team needs to take corrective action to close the gap. Consider an airplane flying from point A to B. Before the flight takes off, the destination coordinates are entered into a computer, and the pilots can calculate how long the flight will take. However, if there are head or tail winds or turbulence, the pilots will need to take corrective action. Similarly if you are driving and have a GPS, you would enter your destination, and the GPS would calculate the best route to take. However, if there are detours on the way or you decide to deviate from the route laid out, the GPS needs to recalibrate and establish how best to get you back on track to your destination. The same thing occurs with goals and targets; the team needs to evaluate whether they are on-plan or need to make adjustments.

Activities are the monthly, weekly, and daily tasks that must be undertaken and completed in order to achieve the target. This is "where the rubber meets the road," in the form of daily to-do lists and tasks that each individual in the team is assigned to carry out.

A key to getting the strategic plan executed is to break up the various, required activities and tasks and assign responsibility for completing each task. It is important to ensure that responsibility is clearly identified. For each activity, someone must be clearly in charge of ensuring the activity stays on schedule and within budget. When responsibilities aren't assigned, people tend to assume that others are taking care of the problems. Be sure to provide authority along with the responsibility.

A useful activities tool is to set out the goals in a spreadsheet format with the following columns, using a modified SMART acronym:

- Specific goal described
- Measurement parameters described
- Actions to take per activity listed
- Responsible and/or reporting parties identified (Who will be performing the   particular task? Who needs to approve it? Who should be kept apprised?   Who should be consulted?)
- Time frame (deadline) defined

Measurement is critical in order to know whether the targets that were set are being hit, and if not, why not and what needs to be done about it. "If you cannot measure it … you cannot manage it," as the well-known saying goes.

When goals are set, they need to be committed to in writing, using clear and concise language that everyone can understand. And when they are achieved, the team will feel motivated and can shout, "GO TEAM!

Here is a recap of what has been accomplished so far in the strategic-planning process:

- The Purpose of the organization is clearly stated in its Vision, Mission, Values, and Principles.
- SMART, long-term goals have been agreed upon, with one Wildly Important Goal (WIG) and a Big, Hairy, Audacious Goal (BHAG) identified.
- Objectives have been determined for each goal.
- Critical Success Factors (CSFs) have been identified for each objective.
- Critical Obstacles and Barriers (COBs) to each CSF have been recognized and resolved.
- Strategies and tactics have been developed for each goal and objective.

It is time to move on and answer the questions, "How do we do it?" "Who will do it?" "Who will be responsible and accountable?" "And how will we measure the result (as opposed to just the activity)?"

4. How Do We Do It? The next step is finally taking action and, to paraphrase Nike, "just doing it." This is the hardest part; this is where the real work happens, and everyone needs to "roll up their shirt sleeves," "put their shoulders to the wheels," and "apply the elbow grease," or any other metaphor you choose. Tools for "just doing it" include:

- Benchmarking
- Project Management
- Process Management
- Performance Management
- A Balanced Scorecard/Dashboard
- Budgeting and Forecasting
- Cash-flow Management
- Human Resource Management
- Change Management
- Root-cause analysis
- LEAN
- Six Sigma
- Total Quality Management (TQM)

Benchmarking and project management will be discussed here; however, each tool is really the subject of its own book.

Benchmarking is the process by which businesses or organizations compare their products, services, and/or practices against recognized leaders with regard to a particular aspect or process. It is possible to benchmark as follows:

- To other parts of your organization or divisions or stores within your organization. For example, how does one store or branch compare to a similar store in the chain?

- To other organizations or competitors in the industry. Walmart may benchmark against Target; Honda against Toyota; RBC against CIBC, and so forth.
- To companies that have similar processes but not within the same industries or sectors. For example, if the speed of a completing a process is vitally important, then a fire department may want to benchmark against other emergency services such as ambulance services. A Tim Horton's or McDonald's drive-through may want to compare its processes to FedEx or a hotel check-in process. Or if you think "outside the box", benchmark against a Formula One Racing Team's pit-stop processes where every second counts. When a race car pulls into the pits, all four tires are changed, the car is re-fuelled, new spark-plugs are fitted, the driver gets a drink…all in less than a minute!
- If customer service is essential, an enterprise may benchmark against companies renowned for their customer service, such as the Four Seasons hotels or Nordstrom department stores. If innovation is important, a company may benchmark against Apple. If quality and reliability are key, then it may be useful to benchmark against Mercedes Benz or Audi.

Determine which critical process you are looking to improve (e.g., speed, customer service, or quality) and benchmark against a business that is known to be the best-in-class in that particular process.

There are various logical steps when benchmarking:

- Analyse and understand your own processes first.
- Choose the process you want to benchmark.

- Select and train the team who will do the benchmarking. Arrange and conduct a site visit with the organization being benchmarked.
- Determine what gaps exist between your process and their process.
- Implement the changes you have learned.
- Be prepared to reciprocate and share your best practices with the other organization.

There are several keys to successful benchmarking:

- Make sure you have a clear benchmarking philosophy with regard to what you are trying to improve.
- Ensure that your people are empowered to implement the best practices learned.
- Become what Peter Senge called a "learning organization"; constantly learn to improve your processes.
- Don't see your business or organization as being unique.
- Benchmarking is an ongoing tool, not a one-shot initiative.
- Exercise with your team by brainstorming about which businesses would be ideal to benchmark against, either within your industry or against similar businesses in different industries.

Project Management brings together and optimizes the resources necessary to successfully complete the project. The first step is to agree on what a project is. A project is an undertaking that has a beginning and an end, and is carried out to meet established goals within cost, schedule, and quality objectives. It is not a permanent endeavour or ongoing work unit, but rather an initiative that results in the creation of a product or service or the achieving of a goal.

The resources involved in project management include the skills, talents, and cooperative effort of a team of people; facilities, tools, and equipment; information, systems, techniques, and money. These resources are used to plan, schedule, and control the project activities that are needed to accomplish the goal. Most members of an organization spend at least half of their time on projects.

Each project moves through a predictable cycle of four phases:

1. Conceiving and defining the project
2. Planning the project
3. Implementing the plan
4. Completing and evaluating the project

Conceiving and Defining the Project. A project is born when someone—the project initiator—decides to resolve a problem or to pursue an opportunity. Project initiation is usually performed by senior management, and all the information about the project would be at a very high level in terms of scope.

At this time it is important to create a project charter, which is a document that formally authorizes the project. The project charter articulates the business need and appoints a project manager who will be given the authority, resources, and responsibility to carry out the project.

There are many reasons to initiate a project, such as:

- Construction or renovation
- Relocation
- Launch of a new product or marketing program
- Process improvement
- Generation of cost savings or increased profitability

To avoid confusion about important aspects of the project, there should be full discussion among the project manager, client, and project team (which may be a cross-functional) from the project's inception.

Leading with four W-questions and one H-question can be useful:

- What is the project that needs to be delivered?
- Why does it need to be delivered?
- When does it need to be delivered?
- Who will participate in the project?
- How will the project be enabled and delivered?

The following sequence of activities will ensure that the project gets under way smoothly:

1. Study, discuss, and analyse the project to ensure that you are addressing the right problem or pursuing the real opportunity.
2. Write a preliminary project definition.
3. State the end-results objective of the project.
4. List both the imperatives and the desirables for the project to be considered successful.

5. Generate alternate strategies that might lead to the objective. Use of free-form, blue-sky brainstorming can be useful in generating ideas.
6. Evaluate the above, alternate strategies.
7. Choose a course of action that will meet the project definition and the end-result SMART goals.

However, before moving to a full-scale project, a feasibility study could be carried out to test the preliminary strategy and determine if it will work, Depending on the nature of the project, it may require a market study, a pilot test, or even a computer simulation.

During the project, management needs to focus on three basic parameters:

- Quality and Specifications
- Cost and Budget
- Time and Scheduling

Planning the Project. Planning is an essential part of project management and requires listing in detail the steps necessary to successfully accomplish a project along the three dimensions of quality, time, and cost. A project plan should be put in writing with necessary approvals and should be used as a tool to manage the project on a daily basis.

The following are important steps in the planning process:

1. Determine the project objective.

2. Choose an approach or strategy for achieving the objective.

3. Create a "scope statement."

4. Break the project down into subunits or steps that identify all the activities that are required to complete the project. This is called a Work Breakdown Structure (WBS).

5. Specify the performance standards for each step, such as quality of materials, tests to be met, and the like.

6. Specify how much time will be required to complete each step to determine the duration of each step.

7. Specify the best sequence for completing the steps, showing the earliest time the step can be started and the latest time it must be started. Here it is useful to create a horizontal bar chart that graphically displays the time relationship of the steps in the project. All the steps are shown in sequence on the vertical or y-axis and the time estimates (in days or weeks) on the horizontal or x-axis. This is known as a Gantt chart (named after Henry Gantt, an industrial engineer who developed the procedure in the early 1900s; see the sample Gantt chart, below). When completed, the Gantt chart will outline the flow of activities in sequence as well as those that can be under way simultaneously. Another useful visual tool for projects with many interactive steps is called a PERT diagram (Project Evaluation and Review Technique) which shows the activities (shown by arrows) that take place between various events (shown in circles).

**Gantt Chart
for Building
Home**

**Steps
y-axis**

7 Lay the
foundation.

6 Order the
cement.

5 Dig the
foundation.

4 Do costing and
quantitative study.

3 Hire the
contractors.

2 Get building
permit.

1 Design
architectural plans
and blueprints.

**Time
x-axis**
(months)
    1   2   3   4   5   6

8. Specify the cost of each step and summarize in the project budget. Typical cost components include labour, materials, supplies, rentals, administrative costs, allowance for overheads, and, if applicable, the desired contribution to profits. The issue of budgeting is a whole topic in itself. However, for the project, some points to consider include whether there will be any impact due to inflation or fluctuation in currency-exchange rates for longer-term projects; whether price commitments are firm or have escalation clauses; variations in estimates made using different methodologies; and allowance for errors in estimates.

9. Determine team needs and the roles and responsibilities of each member; create a responsibility chart showing who is accountable for completing each step and by when.

10. Determine what training each team member may need.

11. Develop necessary policies and procedures.

12. Create a change-control system for any deviations from the original project specifications.

Implementing the Plan. During the implementation phase, the project manager coordinates all elements of a project. This involves controlling work in progress and establishing standards for the project specs that were created in the planning stage for quality, time, and budget. Various charts are useful for project control; they include the following:

- The control point identification chart (CPI), which has a row each for quality, cost, and timeline, and three columns for asking these questions: 1) What is likely to go wrong? 2) How and when will I know? 3) What will I do about it?

- The project-control chart (PCC), which, for each subunit, compares both actual cost and scheduled time with the budget, and calculates the variances.
- The milestone chart (MC), which provides a summary of scheduled completion dates and actual completion dates for each subunit.
- The budget-control Chart (BCC), which shows two lines on a graph; one depicts cumulative actual costs and the other cumulative budgeted costs on the y-axis, over time lapsed on the x-axis.

Controlling work in progress also means monitoring the work in progress, by conducting inspections, interim progress reviews, testing, and audits.

As a project progresses and performance is monitored, there will be times when reality does not measure up to plan, and that is when corrective action must be taken. The project manager must provide clear and timely feedback, both positive and negative, to those who are involved in completing the project; negotiate effectively for materials, supplies and services, and resolve differences using effective problem-solving (win-win) techniques that blend assertiveness and cooperation.

Completing and Evaluating the Project. The client, whether internal or external, needs to accept the project result by agreeing that the quality specifications of the project parameters have been met. Toward that end, it is useful to have a project-completion checklist. If changes were made, the contract must be amended to list the changes in the specifications along with the resulting changes in schedule and budget. The project may not be complete until documentation requirements such as operations manuals or drawings are delivered or people are trained to operate the new facility, equipment, or product. All administrative details need to be finalized.

When the project is complete, the project-team members will need to be reassigned and surplus equipment, materials, and supplies disposed of.

A final step of any project should be an evaluation review by the core project team. This is a look back over the project to see what was learned that will contribute to the success of future projects.

Benchmarking and project management are two very useful, top-of-the-mind tools. For those who want to research further, other tools such as LEAN, Six Sigma, and Change Management are not to be overlooked.

Force Four: Planning

Summary

Planning is essential for the successful achievement of the Purpose of the organization. There is a very true saying: "If you fail to plan, you plan to fail." The overarching plan is called the Strategic Plan which critically evaluates the organization's current strengths and opportunities, what are the top three to five goals that the organization wants to accomplish over the next few years, and how it will achieve these. This forms the foundation for annual business plans and budgets, deciding which projects will be undertaken, which tools will be used to improve operations, and how the organization will keep score and measure success.

Action Items

1. Your team needs to take the time to develop a realistic Strategic Plan starting with a "where are we now" SWOT and PESTLE analysis
2. Use the "GO TEAM" mnemonic to determine "what you have to do to get there"
3. Create three to five SMART Goals, your BHAG, determine your WIG, CSF's and COBs
4. Use tools such as benchmarking, project management, performance management, change management, LEAN and Six Sigma
5. Use a Balanced Scorecard or a dashboard that keeps track of the key performance indicators.

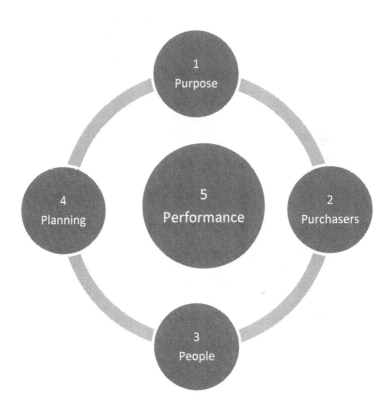

Chapter 5

Force Five: Performance

The end result of the four steps that we have taken is, of course, the "Performance" of the business or organization. Measuring performance enables a business or organization to determine how well it has done in achieving its purpose, serving its purchasers, employing the people who run and help operate the business and who are responsible for the long-range strategic and operational planning. Performance can be measured in a variety of ways depending on the type of business or organization involved.

For-Profit Businesses

Traditional Financial Statements. Financial results are summarized in traditional, accounting-oriented, financial statements and reports. Some examples are balance sheets, which show assets, liabilities, and the owners' equity; income statements (aka Profit and Loss or P and L statements), which show revenues, sales, cost of sales, gross margins, expenses, and any net Income or loss (the "bottom line"); statements of changes in financial position or statements of cash flows; and (specific) statements of owners' equity.

Other Measures. There are numerous financial measures that can be used to assess performance by comparison to prior years or periods, the budget, competitors, or benchmarked businesses. These financial measures include:

- Revenues
- Gross Profit
- Earnings before Interest Taxes, Depreciation and Amortization (EBITDA)
- Earnings before Interest and Taxes (EBIT)
- Earnings before Tax
- Earnings after Tax (EAT)
- Earnings per Share (EPS)
- Price per Earnings (P/E) Ratio
- Net cash flow
- Budgets and variance analysis
- Various other ratios and reports, such as:
  - Working capital (current assets minus current liabilities)
  - Working capital ratio (current assets divided by current liabilities)
  - Quick ratio (current assets minus inventory divided by current liabilities)
  - Inventory turnover ratio
  - Accounts receivable turnover and number of days invoice is outstanding
  - Current assets to fixed-assets ratio
  - Debt to equity ratio
  - Debt to assets ratio

Productivity and efficiency measurements include:

- Output or revenue per employee
- Employee turnover ratio

- Absenteeism statistics
- Break-even analysis
- Cost-volume-profit analysis
- Sales per square foot (for retailers)
- Advertising spent (ad-spend) as a percentage of revenues
- Net-promoter score measuring customer loyalty

Not-for-Profit Organizations

This includes hospitals, schools, charities, other organizations that are designated as not-for-profit (NFPs), and non-profits that are referred to as non-governmental organizations (NGOs). Measures include:

- Traditional financial statements as described above
- Stakeholder satisfaction
- Making-a-difference/"Cause" measurements
- Balanced scorecard Measures
- Meeting-budgets reports
- Percentage of revenues spent on administration versus spent on the purpose or cause of the organization

Governments

This designation applies to all levels of government—federal, provincial/state, and municipal (including police services, ambulance and fire departments, schools, libraries, community centres, etc.)

Traditional financial statements as described above

Citizen-satisfaction polling (ultimately expressed by a vote in an election)

Gross Domestic Product (GDP)

Growth in the economy

Inflation rate

Employment rate

"Great place to live, work, and raise a family" criteria

Balanced scorecard

Balanced budgets

Achieving public-policy objectives

Efficiency measures

Accuracy measures (Six Sigma)

Waste measures (LEAN)

Taxes:

- Income tax rates—effective and marginal rates
- Property tax mill rates

- Value-added tax rates (Harmonized Sales Tax, HST and Provincial Sales Tax, PST)
- Employee Health Tax (EHT)
- Workers Compensation rates
- Consumption taxes, e.g., gas tax, airline tax, and so-called sin taxes such as cigarette and liquor taxes

The objective of performance measurement is to encourage and gauge continuous improvement, growth and sustainability. If an organism or an organization doesn't grow, it eventually ages, withers, and dies. Most businesses have corporate life cycles, and few can survive forever; they are eventually overtaken by innovation, competitors, and change. Accordingly, the objective of performance management is to keep the business or organization relevant, competitive, and vital.

Employees

Performance management and performance appraisals are an essential part of annual and quarterly reviews of everyone in the organization. Performance appraisals allow managers opportunity to develop their direct-reports, make them feel that they are appreciated and valued, and, at the same time, give them feedback as to how performance may be improved.

Although managers and employees alike tend to complain about performance reviews, the reviews do generate meaningful feedback and help with learning, development, and productivity. If done properly, they can offer benefits for all parties involved and be effective motivators.

There are also five P's to consider with regard to successful performance reviews.

Preparation
The appraisal process requires that both the managers and their direct-reports prepare for the performance review well in advance.

Policies
Does the organization have a policy as to deadlines for quarterly, semi-annual, and annual reviews? Are there any prescribed forms that need to be completed?

Purpose
All parties need to understand the purpose of the reviews, which may include evaluation of pay package, career development and promotion, succession planning, and so forth. All parties must understand the link between individual performance and organization results.

Planning

As with everything, planning is key. Managers need to understand the employees' strengths, weaknesses, opportunities, and threats (SWOT), which will include performance gaps that may exist and what the employees' goals are for the upcoming year. Clear expectations must be in place for all employees, going forward.

Process

The performance process should reassure the employee that the performance review will be a two-way conversation and will not become a lecture. Effective performance reviews are coaching sessions in which the manager speaks honestly and openly about the employee's performance, strengths, and goals. The conversation can include information about career opportunities available to the employee and how much development would be required, so that the whole encounter is a positive experience. The manager should also clarify how the employee's progress and performance will be measured and evaluated in the next period.

Force Five: Performance

Summary

In the final analysis, it is Performance that counts. However, Performance may mean different things to different types of organizations on whether it is a for-profit business, a public or private company, a not-for-profit organization, an NGO, a healthcare provider or a government. And the People running these organizations will also be measured and evaluated differently. But regardless of the nature of the organization, just as in sports, performance and measurement are critical for success. It has been said: "If you cannot measure it, you cannot manage it." You must decide what successful performance looks like so that you and the People in the organization know if you are making progress towards achieving your Purpose.

Action Items

1. Determine what success and desired **Performance** looks like
2. Use financial and managerial accounting measures, budgets and variance analysis to keep track of how the organization is doing from a financial point of view
3. Use customer satisfaction and loyalty measures such as Net-Promoter Score
4. Use productivity and efficiency measures to determine employee statistics such as employee turnover ratios, absenteeism, and output per employee
5. Implement a regular and effective employee performance management and appraisal system.

Chapter 6

The Big Five Forces of Business

Summary

This book has presented a mental model or framework of the Big Five Forces that all businesses and organizations need to focus on with a clear line of sight from the desk of the CEO to the work area of every frontline employee.

The Big Five Forces that need to be identified, integrated, harnessed, fine-tuned and focused upon in every business or organization, whether for-profit or not-for-profit, private or publicly owned, or government and regardless of the sector or industry or business cycle, are the following:

1. Purpose

2. Purchasers

3. People

4. Planning

5. Performance

It is my sincere hope that The Big Five Forces of Business will serve as a top-of-the-mind mental-model or framework that will be useful to you and your team as you continue to build your successful business or organization. I hope that it helps you to grow a great enterprise with which you, your customers, employees, suppliers, stakeholders, community partners, and even your country and beyond can be very proud to be associated.

I wish you good luck and success on your journey.

Appendix A.

A-Z Business Topics

- Accounting, Auditing, Advertising, Aptitude testing, Assessment, Arbitration, Appreciative Inquiry, Assertiveness
- Business, Bookkeeping, Budgeting, Balanced Scorecard, Brainstorming, Board-of-directors governance, Behaviours theories, Body language, Benchmarking
- Customer-service, Communication (oral, written body language, listening email), Change-management, Crisis-management, Coaching, CSR, Contract law, Corporate culture, Creative thinking, Conflict resolution,
- Decision-making, Delegating, DISC
- Excellence, Entrepreneurship, Environmental-stewardship, Employee-engagement, Economics (macro & micro)
- Finance, Feedback, Facilitation skills, Forecasting
- Goal-setting, Governance, Gap analysis, Game theory, GANTT Charts
- Healthy-workplace, Health & Safety, Human Resources, Human Capital, Humour in the workplace, Holistic systems
- Interviewing skills, Innovation, Information management, IT, Internet, Intrepreneurship, ISO 9001, Influencing People
- Just-in-time management, Job analysis,
- Kaizen, KISS principle,
- Leadership (numerous models), LEAN, Law (corporate), Contracts, Listening skills, Lease negotiation

- Management, Marketing, Motivation, Mentorship, Meeting-management, Measurement, MBO, MBWO, Mergers & Acquisitions, Mental health in the workplace, Mediation, Morale-building, Mission statements, Mind-mapping
- Negotiation, Not-for-profit directorship & management, Needs analysis, NLP
- Organizational behaviour, Objectives, Outsourcing
- Purpose, Planning, Policy, Process-improvement, Problem solving, Performance management, Project management, Procurement, Public Relations, Public-speaking, Presentations, Power of Positive Thinking, Psychometric testing
- Quality-management, Quality-improvement, QMS, Questions (power of)
- Re-engineering, Restructuring, Relationships, Risk management, Rapport-building, Recognition & Rewards
- Strategic Planning, Strategic Thinking, Strategy, SWOT, Systems thinking, Sales, Six Sigma, Stress-management, Statistics, Social Media, Success-strategies, Self-Management, Securities Regulation
- TQM, Time-management, Team-building, Teamwork, Talent management, Trust-building, Taxation, Tactics, Technology
- Uncertainty, Union-relationship management
- Visioning, Voice-of-the-customer, Variance-analysis, Verification
- Wellness, Writing effectiveness, Work culture, Waste-management, Win-Win Tactics
- "You-Got-It" Superb Customer Service

Made in the USA
Charleston, SC
28 March 2015